revised edition

FURNITURE REFINISHING AT HOME

Nina Glenn Joyner

Copyright © 1961, 1975 by Nina Glenn Joyner

Revised Edition   All Rights Reserved

Published in Radnor, Pa., by Chilton Book Company and simultaneously in Ontario, Canada, by Thomas Nelson & Sons, Ltd.

Designed by Adrianne Onderdonk Dudden
Manufactured in the United States of America

Library of Congress Cataloging in Publication Data

Joyner, Nina Glenn.
  Furniture refinishing at home.

  Includes index.
  1. Furniture finishing. I. Title.
TT199.4.J68   1975   684.1'0443   74-28061
ISBN 0-8019-6144-0
ISBN 0-8019-6145-9 pbk.

To My Fabulous Family
Claude
Glenn
Courtney
Who Never Had a Moment's Doubt

Preface

This is a book written for the amateur—only in the sense that amateur means non-professional. Just because one is not paid for a job does not mean that he cannot do work of professional quality.

It is hoped that this book will be of help especially to the young marrieds and apartment dwellers who may feel that a lack of money or space would preclude their being able to refinish a potential treasure which they might pick up at an auction or garage sale.

Acknowledgments

All of the new line drawings in this book were done by Charles Crouch of Bentleyville, Pennsylvania. He is an excellent artist, and I do not believe anyone could have done a better job. The cartoon in Chapter 14 was contributed by Courtney Joyner of Sewickley, Pennsylvania. Many of the drawings and photographs are reprints from the first edition of "Furniture Refinishing at Home." These were produced by Rose Kirkpatrick and Peter Dechert of Philadelphia. The new photographs are by Ken Balzer and James Shoener from the Pittsburgh area.

Others who helped in many ways toward the completion of this book were Joseph Montello who contributed so much of his time and effort in doing the unglamorous leg work that is always involved in the production of a book. Mrs. Margaret Mutschler, who has a fine antique shop in Leetsdale, Pennsylvania, deserves very special thanks for her useful information and for many of the articles which were used in the "before and after" photographs.

The only way I know to thank my family is to dedicate this book to them with love for the super enthusiasm in never doubting for a moment its completion and success.

N.G.M.J.

1 Why, What, and When to Refinish 3
What Does the Amateur Refinish? 6
What Doesn't the Amateur Refinish? 8
When to Paint Instead 11
Finishing Unpainted Furniture 11

2 Setting Up a Work Area 13
Finding a Good Spot 11
Lighting and Storage 16
Basic Tools and Supplies 19

3 "Taking Down" a Piece of Furniture 23
Tools and Supplies Needed 24
Getting Started 28
Washing with Soap 29
Using a Remover 30
Washing with Shellac Solvent 32
Sanding 32
Making Repairs 33
Refinishing the Dry Sink 35
    Drawers 35
    Hardware 36
    Doors 37

4 Restoring a Natural Finish 39
Wax-Shellac Finish 39
Oil Finish 42

5 Painting and Antiquing Furniture 43
Decorating with Painted Designs 46
Using An Overtone or Antiquing Glaze 49
    Applying the Overtone and Varnish 50
Using Antiquing Kits 51
Painting Without the Overtone 52

6 Brass and Iron 55
Brass Hardware and Trim 57
Brass Beds 58
Iron Furniture 59
    Iron Beds Trimmed With Brass 59
    Wrought Iron Furniture 60

7 Mosaics 61
Mosaic Supplies and Materials 62
Where to Begin 66
Preparing the Tiles 66
Edging 68
Using Antique Tiles 69

8 Picture Frames 72
Materials for Refinishing 74
Restoring the Frame 74
Regilding the Plaster 76
Wood Veneer Frames 77
Using Plaster and Gold Leaf Over Solid Wood 78
Unpainted Frames 79

Contents

9   Trays, Wastebaskets, and Small Furniture   81
Decorating Trays and Wastebaskets   81
    Decoupage   82
    Painting with a Design or Stencil   86
    Using Decorative Fabrics   89
Using Decoupage on Small Furniture   91

10   Lamps and Other Accessories   94
Restoring Old Lamps   94
Making Wooden Lamps   97

11   Chairs   99
Wicker   99
Cane   100
Rush   103

12   Protecting Refinished Surfaces   105
Protective Finishes   105
    Decorative Synthetics   106
    Marble   108

13   New Materials for Refinishing   110
Stains and Varnish   111
Paints   112
Tiles and Plastics   112
Metal Polish   113
Glass and Ceramic Cleaner   113

14   Identification of Woods   114
Cedar   115
Cherry   115
Mahogany   116
Oak   116
Poplar   117
Sugar Maple   117
Walnut   117
White Pine   118
Yellow Pine   118
Curls and Burls   119

15   Care of Antiques   120
Helpful Hints   121

Index   123

Furniture Refinishing at Home

"Wood . . . hidden glories waiting for the touch of craftsmanship and hands that know the loving touch of tools"
John R. Richardson

1
Why, What, and When to Refinish

Refinishing furniture can be a pain! It is nearly always dirty, and it can be hard. The home refinisher ends up with sawdust in his hair, varnish fumes up his nose, gunk under his fingernails, and an absolutely magnificent piece of furniture that most of the time makes the labor worthwhile.

Antique furniture is expensive, and antique furniture in good condition is almost prohibitive in price for the average individual. The slim wallet—rather than a burning desire to scrape paint—is almost always the primary reason for refinishing furniture. Usually, one does not first make the decision to refinish and then start to search for furniture. More than likely one finds a bargain table, chair, or chest at a garage sale, or an auction, in a second-hand store, or inherits a piece from dear old Aunt Maggie.

Anyone who starts out to refinish furniture has to be the

world's greatest optimist. The optimist just *knows* that if he perseveres, he will transform his "piece of junk" into a real thing of beauty.

Before starting a refinishing project, there are a few fundamental requirements for making the restoration worthwhile for even the most optimistic optimist. Without first fulfilling these requirements, the whole project may be lost before it ever gets off the ground. All that time and energy, all those nicked fingers, all those marvelous swear words you thought you had forgotten would be wasted.

Fundamental no. 1 says that almost anything, whether old, new, or middleaged, can be refinished if the basic design is good. Whether the piece in mind is furniture—a chest of drawers, bed, table, cupboard, chair, you name it—or an accessory of some sort (here, the possibilities absolutely boggle the mind) this same fundamental of good design applies.

Now you might ask, "Tell me Ma'am, just what type of household accessory may I refinish?" I will tell you that you are not limited to wood only; you will find that plaster, tin, bronze, brass, copper, marble, almost any conceivable material, whether man-made or natural, is refinishable.

Picture frames are great favorites with refinishers— particularly for the first time optimists, because a picture frame can be small, and it certainly does not have turned legs or worn out drawers. It is better not to start with a life-time project for your first attempt at refinishing. Many an ancestral photograph which once occupied a frame stored in the attic is still intact, but the frame now has been refinished and holds a mirror over the living room mantle.

Other accessories that are great for refinishing are lamps, trays, wastebaskets, and old dough bowls if you are lucky enough to find one. The possibilities are only as limited as the refinisher's imagination (which must be unlimited or he would not be refinishing furniture in the first place). Actually, aside from lack of money (which most people prefer to keep aside) an ingenious rampant imagination is the primary reason that the majority of people ever become embroiled in such a tough hobby.

Fundamental no. 2 is the rule that absolutely requires one to be a *smart* optimist. This rule says that you must have the ability to recognize the possibility of a future treasure hidden underneath a coat of garish paint or behind some elaborate Victorian trim that more often than not can be removed with just a ready hand and a screwdriver.

As hard as it is to admit, and as dull and uninteresting as it sounds, it is positively imperative for the refinisher to be willing to work and to have the tenacity of epoxy to stick with the project when the treasure of the future has not yet reached the future but has reached only the point of seeming like nothing more than just one great big mess!

It is too bad for everyone who is interested in the subject that this book does not have within its pages a cut and dried magic formula for quick and easy refinishing. If such a magic formula did exist, no book on the subject would be needed. Each job is as individual and personal as the refinisher who holds the sandpaper, and each job must be treated that way.

Not only should each project be treated individually, but most of the time you will find that more than one type of wood makes up a piece of furniture, and each type must be treated in its own way. For the novice, refinishing can be complicated; but with the proper guidance and correct tools, miracles can be accomplished.

The whole point of this book is that refinishing is supposed to be a fun, spare-time hobby or craft and not a full-time occupation. For this reason, rather than a lack of ability or "know how" on your part, progress might be slower than one might wish. In this day and age, leisure time seems to be at a premium.

Yes, indeed, there are *kits;* and "kit"—which used to be one of those three letter dirty words to a real craftsman—may now be used in polite company. One real assistance to the home finisher is the furniture "dipper." This professional is now found in many communities. You can carry any type of furniture to him, and he will strip the furniture of the many layers of paint and charge only a modest fee.

If you have not seen ads for this service in your local paper, check the yellow pages of the telephone book; usually furniture strippers are listed under refinishing. Since the stripping of furniture is really the unpleasant dirty work of refinishing, it may be well worth your time to search out a "dipper" in your community.

Even today, with as many good kits as there are on the

market, it is still perfectly possible to ruin any promising project by using a commercial kit. The main problem is that kits automatically mean generalities. In the case of refinishing an antique, a mass-produced commercial kit cannot begin to replace individual craftsmanship and attention.

WHAT DOES THE AMATEUR REFINISH?

What does the incurable optimistic amateur refinish, finish, or restore? Antique furniture? Yes. Modern furniture? By all means. What about mass-produced unpainted furniture? Absolutely! You can have a ball doing this. If antiques are to be restored or refinished, are ornate cupboards or chests to be passed up just because this is your first project? Must the amateur not attempt a job because the piece has Queen Anne legs or ball and claw feet? Ridiculous!

It goes without saying that some styles of furniture are easier to refinish than others; but if the original purchase price of the article to be restored is not prohibitive (and for antique furniture in bad need of refinishing, the price rarely is) and if the end result will blend happily with the decor of the home, then by all means give refinishing a try.

In the field of antique "country furniture," dry sinks enjoy great popularity in this modern day for use as housing for stereos, as bars, or simply as storage units, with the sink's well often being used as a planter (Fig. 1-1).

Because of an actue shortage of storage space in most apartments, many people like to refinish huge armoires and blanket chests. The list of possible types of antique furniture for refinishing could go on and on and on and on some more. There are tables of all descriptions, wash stands, benches, beds, chairs, even all kinds of buckets, pails, and bowls which go along with the popular phrase, "If you can't make a lamp out of it, make a planter."

Modern furniture is particularly adaptable to refinishing. The term "modern" includes all furniture made from the latter part of Queen Victoria's reign up to the present time. Since 100 years is the standard earliest age to qualify as an antique, as we grow older, antiques become younger. One particular era which now qualifies as "nouveau" or "collectable" embodies an especially large multitude of sins. These sins of lacquer and veneer and overdecoration (unhappily, very few were sins of omission) can keep the most avid restorer happily and busily occupied for years to come (Fig. 1-2).

Modern furniture sought for the purpose of refinishing has more than one advantage over antique furniture sought for the same reason. The most obvious advantage is the low cost. Most modern furniture in need of refinishing can be purchased not for pennies, but for very few dollars.

It is not at all unusual to buy a wooden Victorian chair at auction for as little as a dollar. The Salvation Army stores and Goodwill Industry shops are always excellent sources for Vic-

1-1

torian and post-Victorian furniture; and always scan the want ads in the newspapers for the always popular garage sales.

As you know, new unpainted furniture may be bought almost anywhere, but even unpainted furniture can be fairly expensive. Many of the large outlets for unpainted furniture make handsome reproductions of many antiques. It is well worth the price, though, to pay for good design. And the point is *good design* and not necessarily age, unless your interest in antique furniture is purely from a standpoint of investment.

WHAT DOESN'T THE AMATEUR REFINISH?

What does the amateur *not* refinish at home? He positively does not refinish anything at home that he can afford to pay someone else to do for him! With most of us, there are times when if it can't be done at home, it can't be done at all. This book is not about to tell you how hard you must work to refinish a William and Mary butterfly table; because, if you were that lucky to find a true piece of period furniture without having to put a second mortgage on the house, for heaven's sake, do not press your luck by making this treasure your *first* try at restoration. Get a little practice first.

This advice is not to be taken as a slight on your refinishing ability. This is not the case at all. The number one, primary, fundamental difficulty that most amateur refinishers have with true period furniture is not carelessness at all, but rather a

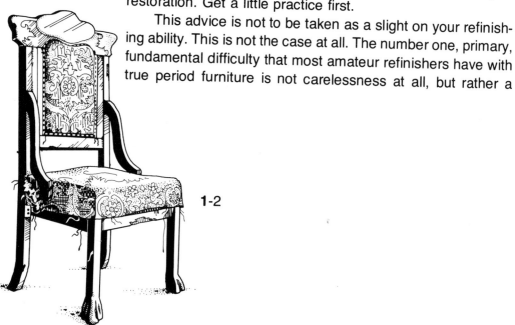

1-2

tendency toward too much care. A fine piece of furniture is ruined just as much or even more by over-refinishing as by sloppy refinishing. If you simply cannot afford to pay a professional to do the job for you now, put the table or chest or whatever in the attic and wait until you have had a little experience to guide you. There is no great rush. Fine period furniture never goes out of style, and time increases its value. This is one move you will never regret. It is too easy for the overzealous amateur to remove completely the beautiful old patina of the wood along with the removal of old paint and varnish.

Never refinish tole! And never refinish certain well-designed handmade furniture—especially if the wood is decent—and it probably is, or the cabinetmaker would never have gone to the trouble to make it by hand. This refers especially to chairs with woven seats such as rush, rope, or corn husks (Figs. 1-3 and 1-4). With daily use, let this type of furniture age naturally and it will acquire a lovely finish all on its own.

At the other end of the pole is the type of furniture that is a pure insult to the sensibilities. We all know there is furniture around today that should never have been made. It was ugly when it was new, and it is even uglier now that it is old. Some of these monstrosities were very expensive when they were bought. (Spending a bundle on ugly furniture is not going to make it beautiful.) There are horrors around that in their heyday were found only in the best homes of some of our "best" people. But as far as design went—forget it!

As an incurable optimist, you might well think that it really is only the black stain that makes a particular piece look so awful. The black stain certainly does not help, but if you paint it white, you will have a big ugly white thing instead of a big ugly black thing. You will have wasted your time and your serene disposition, and you will have ruined the rug trying to clean up the white paint you spilled—and all for nothing. This really is worse-than-nothing because "nothing" does not take up floor space, and it is not necessary to bribe the trash man to carry "nothing" away. Chop the monster up for firewood and be glad to be rid of it.

Use your head when it comes to refinishing. With all the cub scouts, PTA meetings, Saturdays with valued clients, innumerable charity drives, and goodness knows what else that make eating three meals a day and sleeping eight hours a night harder and harder, please try to keep cool and ignore the impulse and do not waste your valuable time on unadulterated junk that even the most highly trained artistic eye and active imagination cannot redeem from a hopelessly poor basic design.

1-3

1-4

WHEN TO PAINT INSTEAD

There are times when it seems the correct procedure is to take a perfectly good antique table or chest of drawers with a fairly decent finish, and . . . do you know what you should do? You should *paint*. You take good heavy enamel, flat or shiny, whichever you prefer, and you cover all the lovely wood with paint.

Many people who have vacation homes and who rent them to others do this. By giving their good antique furniture a coat of paint, this ensures protection of the good wood underneath from scratches and those deadly white rings. When these scratches and rings are neglected, they can be much more damaging to an antique and more difficult to remove at a later date than a simple coat of paint. Certainly, the majority of people do not go in for elaborate furnishings in vacation houses.

It hardly seems necessary to warn you about painting things that either don't need the extra protection or are too fancy to justify the time it would take to remove old paint. For example, while you may consider painting a simple spool bed, don't attempt to paint a sideboard with ball and claw feet.

Usually, there's no need to worry about protecting beds or chairs. On the other hand, it is good to protect flat surfaces which would be susceptible to cigarette burns and rings from wet glasses.

Protecting furniture with paint is one thing, but don't make extra trouble for yourself.

FINISHING UNPAINTED FURNITURE

Unpainted furniture is the greatest invention since you know what! Well-made furniture of this type generally needs only a light sanding before putting any type of finish under the sun on it. Most of this furniture is made from white pine; occasionally you will find walnut, but watch your pocketbook with walnut—black walnut is the most expensive wood available today. In my opinion, it is also the most beautiful; but with the really excellent stains available now, it is always possible to cheat a little bit now and then if you do not insist on putting the brightest light in the room on the "cheating" table.

You must not ever be snobbish when you are refinishing. If your neighbor is putting the finishing touches on an antique walnut frame which you covet (you shouldn't do that you know), go to your local unpainted furniture store; be sure that the furniture is unpainted as well as the store; buy a reproduction for only a couple of dollars, and have a ball producing your own unique "antique."

2
Setting Up a Work Area

FINDING A GOOD SPOT

A much happier thought than deciding where to work is deciding where to carry out your labor of love. Call it love or call it work, it has to be accomplished somehow, and the number one step in refinishing is to map out some sort of program or plan.

Assembling tools and supplies should be the first fun step to come to mind because hardware stores are great on a Saturday morning. By the time you are through visiting with all your friends who have come in for the same thing, you don't have any time left to work. Before you make your attack on the hardware store, decide where you plan to keep all those enticing tools and where you plan to conduct your labor of love.

A good working area is essential to good refinishing.

Good working space does not necessarily mean big working space. After all, many a love affair has gone on in a very small apartment. One must admit, though, that the more room the better.

If you live in a house, the solution to the problem of where to work is obvious—maybe—the basement (Fig. 2-1). Do not use your basement, no matter how light or how roomy, if, at certain times of the year (particularly after a big thaw in January), you need hip boots to get down there or even if the floor is damp. Have you ever tried to use an electric sander while standing on a damp cement floor? I haven't either; that's why I am still here to write about it. If you have a dry basement, you are in luck; but for all our sakes, do not plan to work in the furnace room unless collecting fire insurance is part of your plan.

For some, the attic might be a good working place; but for most, working in the attic does have several disadvantages. Primarily, unless they are exceptionally well insulated (and most are not), attics are sweltering in the summer and freezing in the winter. In most attics, the only daylight that comes in at all filters through a small louvered window at one end. If you like to work at night—and for most amateur refinishers this is the best time to work on a project, outside of weekends—the attic will not do for night work if there are children asleep on the second floor. It is not possible to refinish quietly all the time; there is much more involved than a little quiet painting. In spite of these disadvantages, the attic will do in a pinch if no other space is available.

If you are one of the fortunate ones who live in a new house, there is probably neither basement nor attic; but most new homes have large utility rooms and garages attached to the house. Either of these spots would be ideal. The garage, of course, would not do for wintertime work. Refinishing does not have to take up much space.

Suppose you are an apartment dweller and have no basement, attic, garage, or utility room. Your luck hasn't run out at all. You buy a folding screen to hide the evidence and keep your project in the corner of the living room or dining area. If the piece to be transformed is too large to fit behind a screen, leave the monster out in the open. What visitor could

Setting Up a Work Area 15

2-1

object when he knows that you intend to do something about that "thing" blocking the living room window. Think what a conversation piece you'll have! If there is a small table available, such as a card table, to hold the necessary equipment, it will be to your advantage not to have to reorganize everything each time you decide to work; this would try the patience of a saint. Keep the worktable behind the folding screen (Fig. 2-2).

LIGHTING AND STORAGE

Just for the sake of continuity, let me say here, assuming that a dry basement is to become your workshop, good light is mandatory. Choose your work space near electrical outlets in order to avoid becoming entangled in too many extension cords. Naturally, two outlets would be better than one. If only one light fixture is there, buy a two or three-way socket, but please remember not to use all the sockets at one time. If it is at all possible, buy a fluorescent light that can be easily attached to the ceiling. This will provide you with the best light of all. Don't worry too much if the purchase of the good light takes you over your budget for this one project because the cost of the light will go down and down with each succeeding piece of furniture that you refinish.

Now that you are able to see, the next thing to find and set up is a table large enough to hold all the supplies needed to complete *one phase* of work. A shelf attached to the wall can be used for this if there is not enough floor space for a table.

2-2

2-3

Room enough for just one phase of the work is mentioned because it is ridiculous to have all the tools spread out at one time—the less clutter the better. You will need a cupboard or another shelf to hold the paints, stains, and varnishes that will be needed at a later time.

Where do the screwdrivers, hammers, drills, saws, and other small tools go? You *can* keep them in a drawer or on a shelf, but the most convenient way is to have all hand tools stored in such a fashion that it will not be necessary to paw through a drawer or dig through a messy shelf to find the proper tool at the proper time.

A very popular way of keeping tools is to attach them with clamps to a piece of plywood or pegboard which has been nailed to the wall (Fig. 2-3). The size of the plywood will depend on the extent and variety of your tools. Spacing generously and leaving ample room for each tool, attach metal clamps to the plywood. These clamps have a spring opening and will hold almost any kind of tool. The clamps may be bought in almost every size. Remember, when you go to the lumberyard for your plywood, to ask for "seconds". A perfect piece of wood is not at all necessary for this, and you will save a surprising amount of money this way.

Peg boards are considerably better looking than the plywood-and-clamp method of wall storage, but peg board is more expensive. There is one excellent advantage that the peg board has over the plywood, and this is that the hooks and clamps for peg boards are not attached permanently and can be changed easily as your supply of tools expands.

There is one beautiful way for storing nails and screws, brads and tacks, and nuts and bolts of all sizes and descriptions. Take small jars with screw caps. Nail the caps of the jars to the underneath side of a wooden shelf. Then the jars can be

2-4

attached to the shelf permanently by screwing them to the lids (Fig. 2-4) This idea is by no means original; I have seen it done quite effectively in many home workshops where space was or was not at a premium.

This is an extremely convenient and well-organized way to store nails and such. The more you refinish furniture, the more you will come to appreciate a neat place to work.

BASIC TOOLS AND SUPPLIES

It should be fairly obvious that after all this discussion concerning a good place to work, putting up shelves, and building a clamp board, the next step is to supply the shelves and the board. So the next part of your plan for refinishing is to make another list of the necessary supplies for *this* project, and run—don't walk—to the nearest hardware store. However, do not buy out the store until the need for a certain tool has been established.

Probably the most irritating thing in the world is to be just in the middle of refinishing or restoring a piece of furniture and to find that you need linseed oil or a water-color brush which you do not have. This is particularly annoying if the need for such an article arises as the clock strikes nine and all the stores close. Such a situation will never occur in *your* house because you had your complete list when you first went shopping.

Naturally, different jobs will require different equipment, but there are certain basic tools that will be used on many different projects. These will be mentioned here. The special supplies will be listed at the start of each chapter on the project for which they will be needed.

1. Purchase an electric *orbital* sander (one that goes back and forth, not round and round) or a hand sander and all grades of sandpaper ranging from very fine to coarse. Buy loose sheets of sandpaper not the small pack. These two things are absolutely essential to any refinishing.

What is the difference between the electric (Fig. 2-5) and the hand sander (Fig. 2-6) aside from the obvious? A hand sander can be any flat object around which a piece of sandpaper is wrapped, which will mean smoother and faster sanding than just pushing with the fingers. The best kind of hand sanders are made of cork or hard rubber both of which give resiliency and are normally about 3" x 7" in size, give or take half an inch. Some hand sanders are made of plastic with a little handle on top. Although they are a bit fancier than the cork or rubber, the others are much easier to work.

If it can fit into the refinishing budget at all, permit yourself the luxury of a power tool in the form of a vertical or orbital sander. This electric tool can be purchased for as little as $8 or as much as $30 to $35. If, after inspecting your wallet and discovering that an electric sander will be feasible after all, try to buy one in the $15 to $20 price range. After all, this is a tool which you will be using for a long time to come. The cheapest power tools are not a good investment. If you cannot afford the better power tool, do the job by hand until you can afford the better tool.

Do not use the round sander! Even if you already own this kind of sander as part of an electric drill, do not use it. A round sander will ruin the grain of the wood. You must sand *with* the grain—not across it.

The vertical sander will be your major expense in the purchasing of tools, but it will be well worth the investment in terms of keeping your normally sunny disposition intact. Even with the use of one of these electric marvels, there will be plenty of hand sanding involved. The electric sander is not cheating at all. It is just good sense.

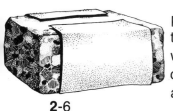

2-6

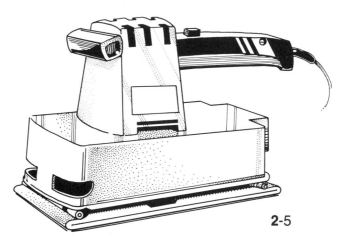

2-5

2. Two more absolutely essential tools are a *putty knife,* or even two of these (they cost less than 50¢;) and, a *paint scraper* (Fig. 2-7). As good as paint scrapers are, this tool will not get into cracks and corners easily. This is why you need two putty knives. There will be dozens of uses for the putty knife besides mixing putty. You will use it for such jobs as spackling, scraping paint in hard to reach areas, caulking, and stirring coffee.

3. Buy several *sponges* just for use in the work area, and also have gobs of *steel wool.* The steel wool which you will buy for refinishing is not the supermarket kind used for scouring pans. This is steel wool just for the purpose of refinishing furniture and comes in grades just as sandpaper does, varying all the way from 0000 to coarse. Buy some of each grade, just as you will buy varying grades of sandpaper. I repeat, *do not confuse this steel wool with the grocery store pads.* Those contain soap. The type of steel wool you require is the hardware store variety.

4. A strong *detergent* such as Lestoil®, Janitor in a Drum®, or Mr. Clean®, a good *paint and varnish remover, turpentine,* and *household ammonia* are essential to your supply of basic needs for refinishing.

5. There are two brands of *glue* which are excellent for use on wood. One is Elmer's® and the other is Sobo®. They are not effective on plastic. There is an excellent new epoxy now available that sets in six minutes. The name of this glue is Quik-i-Poxy®. This can be used successfully on most plastic and fiberglass, as well as all natural substances.

6. A *jack knife, paintbrushes* (several, both 2″ and 1″), and *tooth picks* should complete your list of supplies. You will also want *rags,* in fact as many good clean rags as you can find. You can do without a lot of other things in refinishing, but you have to have *rags!*

7. Be sure that you have the following tools on your supply shelf. They have not been mentioned before because they are found in almost every home. In case you may not have all of them, here they are:

A ratchet screwdriver with small bits for starting holes
A hand drill or small power drill
Ordinary screwdrivers in varying sizes

2-7

Phillips screwdriver
Pliers that will cut wire
A plane
Files in a variety of sizes, including a rat tail file
Hammers in several sizes
A good supply of *single* edge razor blades to use in your paint scraper, among other things

You are now ready to start to work. As previously mentioned, don't begin with too ambitious a project. Select a piece of furniture with plain lines. Size in itself is not likely to discourage a beginning refinisher but intricacy of construction may.

For a start, keep it simple and, without any doubt, many more projects will follow this first one.

3
"Taking Down" a Piece of Furniture

The process of "taking down" (removing the present finish or layers of finishes—and layers rather than one coat is usually the case) is generally used on antique furniture which would be improved by restoration to the original finish.

Before assembling tools and supplies for the process of "taking down" a piece of furniture to the natural wood, make sure that the natural wood is good and the piece itself is worth the effort. Carry a pen knife with you on your antiquing jaunts. No reputable dealer ever objects to having someone scrape a little paint off just to see what is underneath. There obviously is no point in trying to restore a piece to its original finish if the basic wood is not good. However, with most antiques, "taking down" is not only well worth the effort, it is mandatory.

The majority of antiques bought for the purpose of refinishing fall into the category of country or survival furniture. This is not to be confused with true period furniture. You are not likely to be confused by the difference today, as prices for period furniture climb higher and higher. Today a true Sheraton or Hepplewhite or Chippendale large piece such as a desk or chest of drawers is almost non-existent for less than $1,000.

Most country furniture is made of pine, cherry, maple, poplar, or combinations of these. This furniture is simple in design and construction because most of it was made, not by a professional cabinetmaker, but by the head of the family when a new piece was needed in the home (Figs. 3-1 and 3-2).

Although even this type of antique becomes more scarce and, therefore, a little more expensive as the years go by, it still is within the price range of almost every pocketbook. Because you are the incurable optimist and had hoped to find the dry sink or drop leaf table for $60 but discovered much to your dismay that you would have to pay at least $75 or even $100, unless the situation is dire, go ahead and spend the extra money. You know that you are buying an heirloom; you are not buying "early orange crate" which you will be sure to throw in the trash bin in a few years.

As far as the extra $15 or $40 goes, if you spent it at the market for a couple of roast beef dinners, those dinners would be delicious, but how can you refinish old beef bones! Eat beans for a week to make up the difference in what you *planned* to spend and what you *did* spend.

If real early American furniture is what you like in your home, you will have as much fun searching for the original in its unfinished state as you will have refinishing it when you get it home—more fun, probably, because the search is so much easier.

TOOLS AND SUPPLIES NEEDED

This is where the fun begins! This really is *not* where it begins because it really begins when you get the idea to refinish, and it continues when you go hunting for your future treasure, and it continues right inside the hardware store where there is always such an array of fascinating tools, 99% of which you will have no earthly use for. But you can have a ball choosing from the remaining 1%.

3-1

3-2

If you do not already own a *jack knife,* buy this first. *Commercial paint* and *varnish remover* will be essential. Usually buy at least a half-gallon unless the piece to be restored is a small article such as an arrow back chair (if you are fortunate enough to have found one of these treasures) or a foot stool.

Three of these commercial *paint removers* are called Zip-Strip®, Strip-Eze®, and Red Devil®. They are all practically the same—very potent. It would be great if someone would come along and invent a paint remover that would be easy to use and cut down on your labor. All of these products are effective and do the job well but not without some blood, sweat, and tears on your part; that is, unless the object of your labor really is not in such terrible need of refinishing in the first place.

Since all stripping compounds are about the same, and if you feel that the wood in your furniture to be refinished is unusually soft, you either had better leave the stripper on for *half* the time reccommended by the manufacturer or buy a milder paint remover such as turpentine. *Turpentine* on a rag to remove wax and oil, and an *electric sander* to remove a coating of varnish or shellac works beautifully on the softer woods that are not in such bad need of refinishing. White pine, for example, is not hardwood and softens from weathering and age.

Some of the hardwoods are as follows: beech, birch, cherry, chestnut, elm, mahogany, sugar maple, oak, red gum, rosewood, sycamore, and walnut. Pine and poplar both are fairly soft.

Next on your list of hardware store purchases will be *trisodium phosphate* which you will use as well as the commercially prepared paint remover. *Oxalic acid* (available at drug stores) will be necessary if any of the wood in your future heirloom is poplar and needs bleaching. Unbleached poplar is a peculiar greenish color. One pound of oxalic acid is plenty for your needs.

Buy the cheapest medium-size *paintbrush* (2″) and a *paint scraper,* the kind that uses single-edge razor blades. You will need to change the blade often because paint scrapers get so gunky! And—don't forget the all important *putty knife*.

Next, you will need to buy such unromantic and uninteresting articles as an old-fashioned *scrub brush* and a *zinc scrub bucket*. One never knows what some of these super strong chemicals will do to plastic; you just might end up with a hole in the bottom of a plastic bucket and discover that you are refinishing your kitchen floor instead.

Rubber gloves are an absolute requirement. Life is more difficult when working with rubber gloves but not as difficult as trying to work with a scarred hand burned by the stripping materials. The paint removers, your own mixtures and the commercial varieties, are wicked on the skin. Keep a large bottle of ordinary *vinegar* handy just in case the paint remover should get on your skin. Vinegar is a good antidote for alkali burns.

Steel wool in two grades will be used in this dirty business of taking down and in the cleaner job of "refinishing." Buy 0 and 0000 grades; the 0 will be used to help remove the old paint, and the 0000 after the old paint has been removed.

Shellac solvent and sandpaper in all grades are the final items necessary in the process of removing an old finish. When you buy sandpaper, as mentioned earlier in this book, do not buy the small packets. Buy the large single sheets, as many of each grade as you think you will need. Then buy a little more. If you don't use all of it on one job, it will not go to waste as long as it is kept in a dry place.

Remember too, that this list is far from complete for totally equipping a tool and supply shelf. This is a supplementary list just for the job of stripping a piece of furniture of its old paint. However, if you have any money left after buying all the things mentioned here, you might start on the new list of supplies for the new finish.

Obviously, one does not need the supplies for a new finish until the old finish has been removed; but if your work progresses faster than you thought it would, and of course, it will, it might be a good idea to save an extra trip to the hardware store and buy everything at once for the complete job. Refer to Chapter 4 for supplies needed for wax-shellac or oil finish.

No matter how efficient you try to be with all this planning ahead, unless you are a super-organizer, you are going to need one more half-pint of paint remover or just one more piece of steel wool anyway. You probably won't, but you can bet that your friend across town who is doing refinishing will.

At this point, you are likely to be feeling a little grumpy

because of having spent approximately $25 on miscellaneous supplies. You have already put out about $70 on the dry sink, and you don't have a sander. Then you scratch your head and wonder if it might not be good to spend $8.00 and buy the cheapest *sander* which might survive two refinishing projects. Or—would it be better to go all out and spend another $25 on a sander that would last almost forever; or should you rent one.

The first two choices, obviously, are yours alone. No one knows better than you what your budget can stand. The third choice depends on the time you have to refinish. At a dollar or two a day to rent, if you have all day Saturday (most places do not charge rentals on Sunday) and most of Sunday to use the sander and finish with it, so that it can be returned to the store on Monday morning without much expense, then that is the thing to do. On the other hand, if your time is such that you have only a few hours in the evenings to work on your project, and it would take four or five nights of sanding, then you certainly are not going to save money by renting.

Sometimes saving money on tools can be expensive. Saving money on putty knives, scrapers, and even a cheap saw will not hurt anything; it just will not be quite as fast as a more expensive one. Buy a good knife and a good sander. Buy the cheapest paint brushes for the stripping job. They will only be thrown away when you finish. Even though it is a little depressing to have spent so much money for a first refinishing project, keep in mind that many of your purchases will be used again at a later time on another treasure which is just waiting to be refinished!

GETTING STARTED

For a very practical reason, in a first try at refinishing, most people choose some variety of chest of drawers or cupboard. This is the type of furniture that can be used in any room in a house or apartment. At the present time and during the last few years, dry sinks have achieved great popularity among young collectors who do their own refinishing (Fig. 3-3).

One of the best reasons for starting your refinishing career with a dry sink is that all the surfaces are flat. This does make life easier when you can use the orbital sander on nearly the entire surface. There are many reproductions of dry sinks simply because this is such a versatile piece of furniture. Because of its recent popularity, and since it has both doors and drawers, it will be used here for explaining "taking down" and then restoring to a natural finish.

If you have been lucky enough in your treasure hunts through second-hand stores, garage sales, and antique shops to find a dry sink in really rotten condition (which means the price was right) but well designed and built of good wood, then let's not waste any time discussing it—let's get to work!

First, you have to decide where to work. If the weather permits, and you have a yard in which to work, the first steps in "taking down" can be done best outdoors.

WASHING WITH SOAP

Now, grab the hose and a *mild soap* such as Ivory® or Lux®, bring out your brand new scrub brush, and *wash the piece well*. Remove every trace of grease and dirt from all the cracks and corners; now, wash it again. As potent as commercial paint

3-3

3-4

removers are on paint and varnish, they will *not* remove grease and dirt.

If this wash down has to be done indoors for lack of yard space, you will have to substitute a scrub bucket for the hose. One advantage in washing down out of doors, aside from being easier and less messy is that sunlight dries the wood much faster. Sunlight or not, though, be sure that the piece is completely dry after the wash down before actually trying to remove any paint or varnish.

USING A REMOVER

Next, take the can of commercial paint remover and a cheap paintbrush and *slather the dry sink with the remover*. A fairly large area can be coated at one time since this process is messy rather than meticulous. (Fig. 3-4). Since all paint remover cans have small openings, you might want to pour the amount of remover which you think you will need into a coffee can and work from that.

Brush on the remover, which is rather thick, and let it stay on the wood until it begins to have a gummy consistency. This means that it is absorbing paint and varnish. Now, when the remover has reached the tacky stage, don the rubber gloves, take up the paint scraper or putty knife, and scrape off both the remover and paint (you hope). This procedure may have to be repeated two, three, or even four times before most of the paint or varnish comes off. It is best to work from one end to the other and then do each section again rather than completely cleaning the paint from one section, such as a door, before beginning another section. If the entire surface is done simultaneously, the overall effect will be smoother; and if all the wood is the same, one part will not be darker or lighter than another.

If the paint does not seem to be coming off as easily as you think it should with the commercial remover, there is a solution which you can concoct yourself that will take off old paint like nothing else. This solution is never used *instead* of a commercial paint remover. It is used as well as the commercial type when, after having followed the directions for removing paint commercially, you still feel that something else could be done. However, since this mixture is necessarily very potent, great care must be taken in both the mixing and the using of it. Be sure to put the rubber gloves on again.

Take a 2 to 3 gallon zinc scrub bucket, pour in 1 cup of tri-sodium phosphate and add 2 gallons of water. Then, using the scrub brush, wash the remaining commercial paint remover from the article which you are refinishing and brush on your mixture. (Also, do not brush too vigorously or the mixture may spatter—possibly in your eyes.)

This solution will raise the grain of the wood somewhat, so use this only as a last resort. Do not be alarmed by the sight of the raised grain in the wood because even plain water will have the same effect to a lesser degree.

Between the paint scraper and scrub brush, the larger areas should be reasonably clear of old paint by this time. Use the putty knife for removal of paint from the corners and molding. If the piece which you are refinishing happens to have turned legs rather than plain, the trisodium phosphate will be a great help in making the paint removal easier.

WASHING WITH SHELLAC SOLVENT

Now that the paint has been removed, gather up some *clean rags* and wash down the piece again. Only this time instead of washing down with soap and water, you will *wash with shellac solvent*. The shellac solvent acts as an excellent sealer and dries very quickly. At this point you feel that real progress is being made, and it is. Once the stripping is accomplished, the refinishing is fun and does not seem like nearly so hard a job.

If after the stripping, you discover a peculiar greenish wood is stuck right next to the yellow pine, you have one more problem—not a very large problem, but one that needs to be solved before going on to the next step. The greenish wood is poplar, and poplar was very popular in building this type of furniture back in the old days. For one thing it was plentiful; for another it was fairly soft wood which made it easy to carve.

In spite of these advantages, the green color is not especially attractive in appearance and does not lend itself well to staining in its original bare state. To remedy this you will use a solution of *oxalic acid* and water. Mix *1 pound* of acid to *10 cups* of water. Using a paintbrush, apply this solution to the *poplar only,* and let dry in the sun if possible until the wood has been bleached to the desired color. Sunlight quickens the bleaching process, but it is not essential to the effectiveness of the acid.

After the wood has been bleached to your satisfaction, saltlike crystals will remain on the surface. These crystals must be washed off with clear water; when this has dried, sand the wood lightly. Before sanding, *be sure the surface is bone dry* because the oxalic acid will have raised the grain as well as changed the color of the poplar.

Oxalic acid is not magic. It will not transform poplar into pine, cherry, or walnut, but it will surely bring the poplar to a color that will blend much more happily with whatever other wood was used in the construction of the furniture.

SANDING

Even the best use of paint remover, trisodium phosphate, and oxalic acid (if it is needed) will not take the place of a good *sanding*. The paint remover may have cleaned off all the old paint and varnish (more than likely it did not) but the wood surface will be pitted and rough from the use of such strong solutions and scrapers.

The degree of roughness will determine the grade of sandpaper required at this time. Generally the coarse paper is used at first to erase any last particles of paint. The electric sander will be a tremendous help for the larger areas. In the corners you just have to sand by hand.

When the wood surface is completely clean, change to a medium grade of sandpaper for smoothness. If the surface still feels a little rough to you, sand lightly and gently with fine grade paper.

MAKING REPAIRS

If the dry sink is now free from any trim, old paint, and varnish, remove the doors and drawers as well as the lid if there is one. Now is the time to *make repairs if necessary* (Fig. 3-5).

There are arguments for making repairs before stripping. My argument for repairing after stripping is that matching wood is so much easier when you do not have to guess what it is you are trying to match. By removing the old finish first, you help to keep the parts of the unit as uniform as possible. Glue and possibly some *wood filler* will be used in repairing your project, and there is no point in adding to the old finish that needs to be

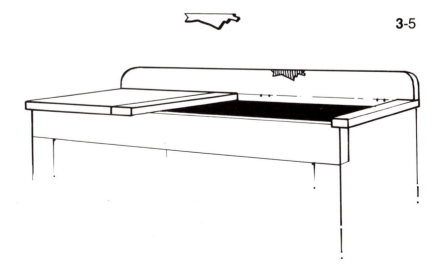

3-5

removed. Why make extra work for yourself? Most of the time the best plan is to take every loose part off the frame of the furniture, in this instance, the dry sink.

Ignore the small nicks and scratches. If you get too ambitious with the wood filler, you will end up with a piece of furniture that will be taken for an excellent reproduction rather than a restoration. Some unscrupulous antique dealers produce their own antiques by hitting the new wood with a chain to make it look old! There are likely to be larger gashes or splits which will require filling. Some of these may be built up with *wood putty*—easy as making mud pies! Real breaks in the furniture will require some of your stockpile of wood to be cut and set in. This procedure is really very easy but does require care.

Obviously, your choice of wood should match as nearly as possible to the wood which you are repairing. Cut approximately to the size of the break, letting your repairing wood be just large enough so that it can be carved to fit nicely without being too loose. Don't be like the man who kept sawing off table legs to make them even and ended up with a great place to play Monopoly on the floor.

A perfect fit for your carving can be made with the use of a file and sandpaper. In using the file, though, for the final shaping of your wood, do not use the coarse side of the file. This kind of shaping can best be done with the fine side. If the repair is small, a rat-tail file is perfect.

If it is new wood that you are carving, the piece will have to be matched in color as closely as possible with the old. A good blending of color is more likely to be the outcome rather than a perfect match. You might want a perfect match in marriage or painting woodwork, but a perfect match is not necessarily the perfect thing in refinishing antiques. Most people, unless they have refinished a great many pieces of furniture, are not fortunate enough to have old wood lying around the house. So, bring on the stains for the new wood. Don't worry about new wood if it has aged enough to be dry. If you repair with green wood you are in trouble because as the moisture leaves the wood, it will shrink.

The commercial stains on the market today are perfectly acceptable in the refinishing of furniture. Glidden's®, Stain 'n Buff®, and Sherwin-Williams® have a particularly wide variety of stains.

3-6

Assuming that pine is the predominant wood in your furniture, buy a small can or tube of dark pine stain and color the piece of wood which was carved to fit the break. If the commercial stain is not dark enough, and it might not be, add a drop or two of *burnt sienna* oil paint (the kind artists use) to the commercial product. Keep on mixing and staining until the nearest possible color to the old wood has been achieved.

Now, the new wood has been carved to the correct size; the color has been matched. Take up your plastic bottle of Elmer's Glue-All or Sobo or Quick-i-Poxy and using any one of these glues, set the wood in place. Remove any excess glue; do not let the milky color bother you, it becomes clear as it dries. Even though the patch job will show, it will not detract in any way from beauty and charm of the finished piece of furniture (Fig. 3-6). It is just this sort of thing which, if done well, can add to the personality of your project. This is your personal stamp!

REFINISHING THE DRY SINK

Drawers

If your dry sink has a drawer or drawers that need no repair, you are one of the lucky few. Most drawers in this type and age of furniture, if they are not actually in pieces, are so loose that you should take them apart and rebuild them. Nearly all have either no pull or an improper one that was added at a later time. This will need to be replaced, but more will be said later on the subject of hardware.

If, in the course of human events, and your refinishing career, you have no worse problems than the rebuilding of a drawer, then thank your lucky stars and get on with the job.

Repair of the drawer itself is quite simple. If you remember that what you are dealing with is a primitive country piece of furniture, you need have no fear of dovetailing (Fig. 3-7) Put the drawer together using glue or nails to hold it. However, be sure that you use headless nails; sink them well into the wood and cover with wood filler. If a piece of dovetailing is missing just fill the hole with wood filler.

Hardware

Hardware is one of the most fun parts of refinishing furniture. The correct hardware is very important. An insignificant little item such as a drawer pull is many an amateur refinisher's downfall. Too many people do a beautiful job of repairing and refinishing a primitive piece and then manage to ruin the whole effect of simplicity with fancy hardware. Try your best to match the hardware to what would have been used originally on the piece of furniture you're refinishing.

Most country furniture including chests, cupboards, dry sinks, and so on had *wooden* knobs for pulls (Fig. 3-8). Brass was used mainly by city cabinetmakers, and glass was expensive. Do not cheat on the style of the dry sink! If the original drawer pull is missing, buy a wooden knob at the hardware store and stain it to match. If the original is not missing, do not change to something elaborate. Putting a brass pull on a dry sink is like wearing a diamond necklace with a bathing suit. When you go to stain the wooden knob which you bought, use the same method as for coloring the carved piece you fitted into the break.

It is so easy to be misled by the most well meaning people when you go to buy the hardware for the cupboard doors. In this case, "hardware" means hinges. Nearly every mass-produced reproduction will show a dry sink or any other primitive cupboard with "H" or "L and H" black hammered iron hinges (Fig. 3-9). These are so wrong for this type of furniture.

Use the *invisible* hinge. The original hinges might not have to be replaced. Even if the originals are rusty, they can be cleaned up with fine steel wool (000) and *machine oil*. Always keep in mind that you are not refinishing a reproduction. What you are putting your blood, sweat, tears, and money into is a fine original piece of furniture, and that is the way you want it to look. Anyone with enough money can have a reproduction. The whole point is that the original *is* original. No one else in the whole world has an antique dry sink quite like yours, and that is why you have to be careful to keep it that way.

Doors

Plan to allow plenty of time for hanging the doors. Sometimes this can be one of the most frustrating parts of this job. What you think looks straight is invariably off kilter.

3-8

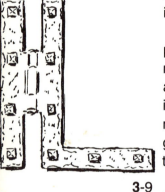

3-9

Before actually screwing the cleaned hinge to the door frame, hold the door in place and mark the edges of both door and door frame with a pencil. These pencil marks will show you just exactly where the hinges should go. After marking both the door and the frame, use small screws and attach the hinges to the *door* first. When the hinge is on the door, hold the door to the door frame and with small screws just barely attach the hinge to the frame at the correct places which you previously marked with the pencil.

There is a very good reason for first going lightly on the screws. Even though the door may seem to hang straight to the frame, the wood is old and may be slightly warped. If the door hangs too straight, it may not open and shut properly. Keep adjusting the door until it moves freely back and forth, and then tighten the screws. Just be patient and keep working and adjusting the position slightly. Don't ever think of planing the edge!

On the door, too, a wooden knob should be used for the pull—no brass, no hammered iron, no glass. Stain the knob to match the door, and if your dry sink or cupboard does not have an outside wooden piece for a lock, buy a magnetic lock to fit inside. These are not really locks but simply magnets which may be attached to the shelf. With epoxy or one of the other glues such as Elmer's you then attach a small piece of steel to the inside of the door, and it will stay shut.

Now, the worst of your work is over, and finally, you are beginning to see some results.

4
Restoring a Natural Finish

Since a natural finish can be used on *new* unfinished furniture as well as on an antique which has been stripped, it need not be considered only for old furniture. After the hard work of stripping and sanding and repairing, this is the beauty treatment.

WAX-SHELLAC FINISH

One more wash-down is necessary whether your project is old or new. This wash-down is not to clean; the purpose of this is to seal the wood. The washing is done with *boiled* linseed oil and turpentine. The proportions of this combination are 1/3 *boiled linseed oil* to 2/3 *turpentine*. The total amount to mix will depend on the size of the piece which is being refinished. Even for something as large as a dry sink, a pint can of boiled linseed oil is sufficient, and you probably will not use all of that. The old scrub brush will not be used for this washing. This preparation of turpentine and oil is applied with soft clean rags. So, bring on the rags!

Do remember that *boiled linseed oil* is a commercially prepared product. Do *not* buy raw linseed oil and try to boil it yourself! The oil is highly flammable. Be sure that what you buy says *boiled* on the label of the can.

After applying this mixture over the whole piece of furniture, take a rest. The wash-down must be allowed to dry for *48 hours*. Although it does seem that it should not take so long, the extra time will give any excess oil a chance to be fully absorbed by the wood. While you are waiting for the next step in your refinishing, postpone your rest while you properly dispose of those oily rags. Do not allow these rags to lie around in a heap. Oily rags left lying around are the best way in the world to start a fire.

After the full 48 hours of drying time have elapsed, take a clean dry rag and wipe over the entire surface to make doubly sure that your project is ready for the next process. If any appreciable amount of oil comes off on the rag, leave the next step for another day. After the wood has soaked up all that is possible for it to absorb, there will still be a very slight oiliness to the finish; just wipe it off.

Now the time has come to apply the shellac solution. The shellac will not be too shiny or too glossy because you will not apply pure shellac to your furniture. You will use *shellac solvent* and *four pound cut shellac*. Even the *cut* shellac will need to be cut three or four more times by you, but this is easily done.

Take a wide-mouthed quart jar with a screw cap—such as a Mason jar—not a milk bottle (nowadays if anyone has a real glass milk bottle, it is more likely to be on a collector's shelf than in the kitchen). You need the wide-mouthed jar so that you may dip a brush into it. Into this quart jar, pour *1 cup* of cut shellac and *3 cups* of shellac solvent and mix well.

Apply this mixture with a clean dry brush just as evenly as you possibly can, and let dry *thoroughly*. Letting this mixture dry completely is the most important part of the entire process. Impatience here will do you in for sure. This process must be repeated not less than 7 times and more than 7 if you have the energy and patience.

Applying the shellac is not difficult, but remember that this is not paint remover which you are using, and do not just slop it on. Be sure that each layer is completely hard and dry before painting on the next layer; otherwise you will have a sticky mess.

Important note: Every other coat (numbers 1, 3, 5, and 7) of shellac which is applied *must be sanded*. For this type of sanding, the very finest grade of sandpaper is used, and it is best to do it by hand. If you think that you are able to use the electric orbital sander without removing your finish, then give it a try.

After the final sanding, number 7 or more, the waxing will begin. There is one brand of wax which professionals highly recommend. This product is Butcher's® paste wax. This wax is not the easiest to use, though, because of its hard finish. There are two other brands that have also been recommended by professional refinishers that are easier to use, but do not produce quite the same effect as Butcher's. These are Johnson's® brown paste wax and liquid Min-Wax.® Most pro's do not feel that a liquid wax does quite as good a job.

Following the applications of shellac and intermittent sanding, the waxing will produce a satiny finish that you would never have believed possible from the appearance of your project when it was first brought into the house.

Apply several coats of wax—the more, the better. Buff hard and well between applications. This buffing does *not* have to be done by hand. If you own an electric buffer use it; if you do not own an electric buffer but have an electric drill, buy the buffer attachment for the drill. They are not very expensive and can be purchased for less than $5. If the buffing is done by hand, be sure that your rags are both dry and clean. Of course, this also holds true for your buffer. Old tee shirts are the absolute best polishing rags of all. Any soft cotton *knit* rag is better than broadcloth or percale that might be part of an old sheet or shirt.

This is the absolute end—the time to admire! Sit back now and look at what you have done. After all the thought and labor that went into your project, you have not only increased the intrinsic aesthetic value, but you have at least doubled the commercial value of the furniture.

Relax a while and start thinking about the next project. Now you know what and how to do it, and the second piece will be a breeze.

OIL FINISH

The wax-shellac finish is not mandatory. Many people prefer a duller finish. The oil finish is the solution for this. It is very simply done and quite effective on most woods.

Only four ingredients are needed for the oil finish mixture: *boiled linseed oil, raw linseed oil, turpentine,* and *varnish.* Mix as much as you will need according to the size of the piece to be refinished, using the following proportions: 1/4 boiled linseed oil; 1/4 raw linseed oil; 1/2 turpentine; add 1 teaspoon of any varnish per quart.

Rub the oil finish mixture on the furniture with a clean rag and *let sit* for about 10 minutes; then wipe off with another clean rag. Do this at least 3 times, but 6 times is preferable. In refinishing furniture, it is always worthwhile to go the extra mile. Allow 24 to 48 hours between coats. When you have finished, do not forget to *throw those oily rags away!*

5
Painting and Antiquing Furniture

The well-known cigarette slogan, "You've come a long way baby!" can be applied most aptly to the antiquing of furniture.

Several years ago, the only sure way of having a professional looking job was to mix your own overtones and do it all from scratch. This is still perfectly acceptable, but it falls somewhat in the category of using a washboard and tub to do the laundry instead of an automatic washer. In some cases it is preferable; I still think a horse and plough are easier to handle than a Rototiller®.

The first decision is not whether to use a kit, but what kind of furniture are you planning to paint or "antique." Number one point is that you never antique an antique. Although, as was discussed earlier in this book, the dateline for the definition of antique changes every year, most people think of real antiques in terms of eighteenth and early nineteenth century furniture.

Late Victorian and early twentieth century furniture was mostly horrendous. This is the type to aim for when you think about painting or antiquing.

This process is preferred also in many instances when the grain or color of the natural wood is undesirable by today's standards, particularly when the natural wood is yellow oak or walnut with a black stain, both of which were commonly used in the larger furniture of the years from the turn of the century until the thirties.

Antiquing or painting is a very popular way of giving an entirely new look and personality to a heretofore really deadly piece of furniture. This method of rejuvenation is used mostly for furniture circa 1910, give or take a few years. The style is familiar to everyone who has grandparents. There are sideboards that are real monsters with huge carved backs on them. The wood is almost impossible to identify from a cursory glance at the outward appearance. This is due to the innumerable coats of almost black "mahogany" vanish. The entire effect of one of these pieces is that of a monstrosity to be rid of at the first possible chance at replacement.

Before giving this indestructible horror to the nearest junkman, give it a second thought (Fig. 5-1). Maybe something can be done about this piece of furniture, not only to make it useful to you, but to make it attractive as well.

5-1

Painting and Antiquing Furniture 45

There is no need to despair over the almost black finish. After all, the incurable optimist that refinishes furniture knows that for every disaster of design, there is no remedy; but for every disaster of finish, there has to be a remedy. In this case, start at the top.

Many of the sideboards of this particular era seem to be topped by a combination mirror, what-not shelf, and hat rack. This can be removed quite easily with the use of your screwdriver. If the back happens to be nailed on, which is not likely, just pry it off. There is really almost nothing you can do to something like this that will make it worse. There might be a little glue aside from the screws or nails, but give a tug and the whole piece will come off. You will not believe the difference this first step will make, and you really haven't done anything yet.

Remove those awful elaborate drop pulls from the doors and drawers. They are as up-to-date as an Empress Eugenie hat. Even without the top and the hardware, you still have a great hulking dark piece of unattractive furniture. But the storage space *is* good, and there is possibility of personality, so the next problem is to figure how you would even begin to lighten and enliven such a reminder of other years.

The answer, in this chapter obviously, is to paint or "antique"; and as always, the first step in this process is to organize the materials. The materials listed below are the necessary ones if you are *not* using a kit though some would also be used with a kit.

1. Medium and fine grades of sandpaper
2. Flat white paint for the base coat
3. Any flat paint in your choice of color for final coat
4. Tube of raw (burnt) Turkey umber—artist's oils
5. Turpentine
6. Clear waterproof *flat* varnish
7. Brushes for paint and varnish
8. Clean soft rags
9. Boiled linseed oil (see Chapter 4)
10. Jar of pumice powder

Once all the necessary materials are handy, and all the unnecessary trim and hardware have been removed from the piece of furniture, the real work is ready to begin. Get out the bucket and sponge and wash the piece well with soap and water. (That step should come as no surprise.) Clean every inch and every corner inside and out and let dry thoroughly. There is no way that anyone can refinish over dirt and grease, and despite your impassioned desire to get going with something that will show results, the wood must be completely dry, for sanding damp wood is a rotten idea.

Sanding follows scrubbing in the preparation for antiquing or painting. This is not hard sanding at all, since it really is not necessary to remove all the old finish as you would with an antique. Only sand the old finish enough so that a primer coat of white paint will adhere smoothly to the old surface. This is one of the super advantages in antiquing.

Flat white paint is always used for the base coat if the final coat of paint is a pastel. The reason for this is that the original surface of a piece to be treated this way is invariably so dark that the original would bleed through any pastel shade without this good heavy white base. Depending on the original finish and the darkness of it, more than one coat of flat white may be required to get the professional look that everyone wants from his labors. After all, you want to have to *tell* your friends that you did it yourself—not have it look that way. There is a world of difference (Fig. 5-2).

The final coat of paint, whether white or pastel, flat or shiny (I prefer the flat look for this type of furniture), must be given a chance to dry thoroughly before attempting to do any painted decorations or overtone. Remember, the overtone *follows* the decorations.

If you want to have just a simple piece of painted furniture, your work is now almost done. To protect the top, sand it lightly with a fine grade of paper and coat it with a flat varnish.

DECORATING WITH PAINTED DESIGNS

Many people like to decorate their furniture with painted designs before antiquing with the overtone. These decorations can include anything from a simple monogram and good accent on the head board of a bed or back of a chair to quite elaborate scenes, very often Oriental in effect, painted on the panels of a

5-2

chest of drawers or sideboard or a desk (Figs. 5-3, 5-4, and 5-5). Any of the larger pieces of furniture are very good for this. If you go "new" furniture shopping today, practically all the better furniture manufacturers have their own lines of antiqued and painted furniture, and it is very expensive. This is another area where doing it yourself more than pays for itself.

If, when it comes to painted decorations on your furniture you find that you are something less than an amateur Rembrandt, all you need is a pattern, and this is easily found. American Handicraft, which has stores all over the United States, has at least two pattern books; patterns can also be ordered from *The American Home* magazine.

Before actually tracing the design for painting, be sure that the final coat of base paint is smooth as silk. This will mean a light sanding with fine paper. After the final coat of paint has been sanded, apply a coat of *flat* varnish and allow to dry thoroughly; this means at least 24 hours in dry weather. The oil paints must not go over a finish that gives the least suggestion of stickiness. Just think of the mess that would be!

The decorations, if put on with oil paints, take a *very* long time to dry. This period is not measured in days or hours—this means *weeks,* not less than two weeks and maybe even three. There is nothing for you to do now but forget the whole project during the drying time. Protect it any way you can during this drying time so that no one bumps against the paint and smears your work.

When you are sure the oil paints are completely dry, coat the entire painted area with flat varnish, or use one of the new spray varnish protectors rather than applying with a brush. This is done to protect the painting when the overtone is applied (Fig. 5-6).

Obviously, if the only painted design used is a monogram in gold leaf paint or oil base paint in a contrasting color, your drying time will be only a day or two, since artists' oils are not necessary for this type of decoration. Although, this, too, must be covered with the flat varnish before doing the overtone or antiquing.

If the gold trim around the edges is done with paint, this must be covered with varnish before antiquing. There is a new product available called Rub 'n Buff® which comes in a tube and, after it has been applied and rubbed on the furniture, looks very much like gold leaf. This may be used *after* the overtone and is very simple to use when the directions on the label are

5-3

Painting and Antiquing Furniture **49**

followed. Aside from a wide spectrum of colors, Rub 'n Buff comes in copper and silver as well as three shades of gold.

USING AN OVERTONE OR ANTIQUING GLAZE

The overtone is the icing on the cake when antiquing a piece of furniture. The recipe for a medium-dark overtone is as follows:

1. 2 tablespoons raw burnt (Turkey) umber
2. 3 tablespoons turpentine
3. 1 tablespoon clear waterproof varnish
4. *Drop* of linseed oil

Squeeze the burnt umber into a jar. Add the turpentine and mix with a brush. Add the varnish and mix well. Finally, add a

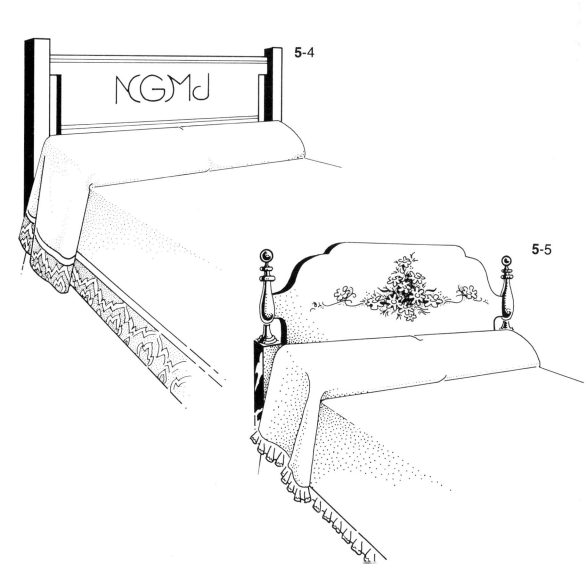

two of the linseed oil. The oil keeps the overtone mixture from drying too fast. Be sure to mix the overtone in the order given above.

Applying the Overtone and Varnish

1. Apply the overtone to the furniture with a 2" paintbrush.
2. Let dry for just a few seconds, not longer than one minute, depending on how dark a finish you want. (Test the color by rubbing on a small spot first.)
3. Wad a soft clean cloth and *rub off* the overtone just applied; do this with a circular motion.
4. The center or top of a panel should be lighter than the sides, so let the darker tones in the corners, cracks, and depressions of the furniture.

When the overtone is first put on, it will probably scare you half out of your wits. It is so black and so "all-covering" that your first reaction when seeing it will probably be a strong desire to throw this book in the garbage pail. Don't panic; as bad as it looks when first applied, it wipes off quickly and easily and leaves a beautiful parchment like appearance that is not dark at all.

The *drying time* for the antiquing is very short. If the over-

5-6

tone is applied at night, then by morning to should be ready for the next step, which is the application of varnish. The flat varnish is painted over the dry overtone for protection of the finish. Even though the antiquing is prefectly dry, each time the furniture would be dusted or wiped off with a damp cloth, a little bit of the overtone would come off, so that after a few months you would be wondering what had become of all your work. One coat of varnish will do, but as always two will be better. The flat varnish will not change the appearance of the decorations or overtone.

USING ANTIQUING KITS

The kits for antiquing that are available today are excellent. The choice of color is almost unlimited, and the glazes are good. If the piece of furniture which you are refinishing is small, there is no need to even consider mixing your own glazes and overtones. Good kits can be expensive to use because a single kit will not cover a large piece of furniture that would need a base coat of paint as well as the final color. These kits average about $5 each; and, obviously, if you are planning to do a complete bedroom in this way, it would be much cheaper to mix your own.

5-7

For very small jobs such as the unfinished wooden box in Figure 5-7, Rub 'n Buff is excellent. (See color insert for finished box.) This costs about $1.30 a tube, and one tube was plenty for the box shown here. There are eighteen colors from which to choose; however, while it is not recommended for tabletops, it is highly recommended for accessories and picture frames.

Almost every paint manufacturer has antiquing kits. Some have them using latex paints as well as enamels. One that is a little more expensive than the others is made by Martin Senour Paints. This company has a kit called Frostique® as well as the standard antiquing kit. Frostique is very light and modern using pastels with a white overtone.

For a different effect from ordinary overtones, try a marbelized finish. First, paint the furniture with a base paint—a flat or high gloss oil base paint in white or pastel. (For this type of finish, a high gloss is better.) For the marble effect use artists' oil paints. Experiment first with a scrap of painted wood. Mix the oil paint with the turpentine until it is the consistency of condensed soup in the can. Then, with a sable brush (artist's brush), apply the paint in globs at intervals of about ten inches. After the "globs" sit for a while, gently join one glob with another using a circular motion with your brush until the marble effect is achieved. When the design is thoroughly dry (after several days), protect the entire painted surface with *spar* varnish.

PAINTING WITHOUT THE OVERTONE

Overtones or antiquing glazes are not called for on all painted furniture. If you happen to be of a more modern frame of mind and want a little less parchment and gold, many attractive combinations of pastel with white (Frostique) or pastel with gold or white with gold can be just as effective as the umber overtone. The type of final finish that you use depends entirely on your choice of furniture and the decor of your home (Figs. 5-8 and 5-9).

Victorian washstands with marble tops have endless possibilities as painted furniture (Fig. 5-10). These washstands are not expensive; however, they are becoming more popular every year and cost more now than they did a few years ago when they could be picked up for a couple of dollars. Those days are gone forever! Now you might have to pay as much as $100 for one in good condition; but since the whole idea is to

5-8

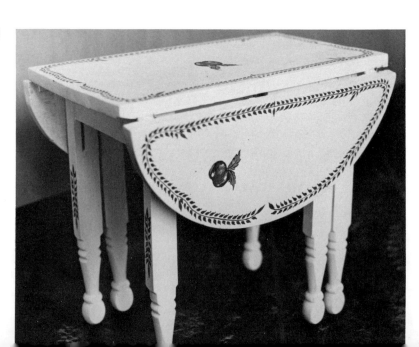

5-9

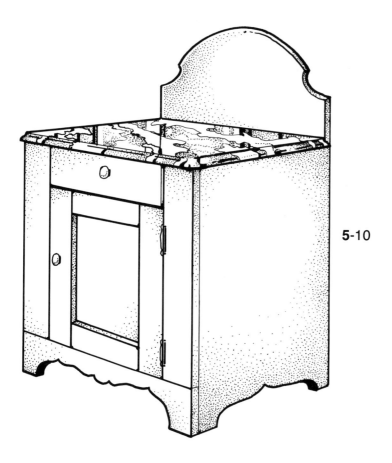

5-10

refinish it yourself, if you keep your eyes open, they can be found for about $25.

These wash stands are great little pieces for the hall or dining room. In fact, one can be used successfully in any room of the house. They make good night tables. Most of the marble tops are white; some are pink marble which is cheaper, but not so versatile. Some even have black marble tops; these can be very effective in a modern room.

6
Brass and Iron

Another successful effort at refinishing has been completed. The last coat of varnish has dried. The time has come to speak of many things—of cabbages and kings—and hardware. This has not been discussed in detail before because your choice of hardware is completely personal and depends entirely on the way in which you finished your piece of furniture.

There is no hard and fast rule for hardware with painted furniture. However, as was mentioned in Chapter 3, there are certain rules to follow with antique furniture that is being restored. With painted furniture, generally, the more elaborate drawer and door pulls look well only on the more elaborate pieces. The plain pulls are better for the plainer furniture. Notice the difference in decoration and hardware on identical secretaries shown in Figures 6-1 and 6-2.

If the final finish is only the overtone over color, then elaborate door or drawer pulls are definitely in order. Now,

many of the smaller hardware stores carry a wide variety of furniture hardware. The lumberyards are also good sources for this. Many antique dealers have catalogs from which you can order practically any type of pull or hinge.

If, however, you happen to live in a smaller community or in the country away from such hardware stores or lumberyards, then the next best thing to do (and sometimes the best) is to order a catalog from a brass and iron works which specializes in small hardware. Two sources for reproductions of this type are the Ball and Ball Brass Works, Exton, PA 19341; and Horton Brasses A. J., Box 95, Cromwell, CT 06416. Horton charges $1 for a catalog. Order your catalogs and brasses during that three week stretch of drying time for your oil painted decorations.

There is much less time involved in the antiquing or painting of furniture than in the restoration of wood to a natural finish, but even a painted finish requires a certain amount of care. Just because you have a monstrosity, or a particularly ugly piece, to start with, the end result can be even more disastrous than the beginning without giving the utmost care to detail.

BRASS HARDWARE AND TRIM

If you are fortunate enough to have an antique with its original brass pulls, there is no need to despair if they are completely black. You're probably thinking there's no commercial polish on earth that will totally remove all the black, but Parson's® *sudsy ammonia* will!

Take a glass jar that is large enough to hold the brass pulls that need cleaning (be sure the jar has a screw cap) and put the pulls or hinges in the jar. Fill with enough ammonia to cover the brass. Put the lid on before you asphyxiate yourself (I have to hold my breath while filling the jar) and let soak for 10 or 20 minutes. You will see the flecks of black come off. After the black is off, remove the brass and wash with warm water. They will not be shining, but they will be reasonably clean.

After the ammonia has been thoroughly rinsed away, you may polish with any commercial brass polish such as Brasso®, and you will not believe your eyes when you see how beautiful those drawer pulls look. If you like, there is a product available called Boat-Nu® which is a spray lacquer that may be used on brass after polishing to prevent tarnish. Boat-Nu does not put a glassy finish on the brass which should have a soft, well rubbed look. There is no way to tell that this spray has been used except for the fact that it prevents tarnish. However, there seems to be an exception to everything. The exception for using the spray to prevent tarnish is on andirons. Heat from the fire will cause most lacquer to peel which means that it then has to be removed entirely, and this is very hard to do.

BRASS BEDS

Brass beds are appearing on the scene again after having been relegated to attics, basements, and junkyards for many years. These beds run the gamut from plain and simple to super elaborate. The prices run the same gamut from less than $100, for one to refinish yourself, to $2,500, for an ornate bed which has been polished for you.

If the bed you buy has been painted as many of them were, unfortunately, the paint is removed with commercial strippers in the same way as from wood furniture. The paint seems a little easier to remove from the brass because there is no grain for the paint to soak into.

As with wood furniture, the same professional furniture "dippers" will clean a brass bed. This is more expensive, but if you picked up a bargain in brass, it might be worth your while to have it cleaned professionally.

The main difference in removing paint from brass and from wood is that you cannot use a sander, since, obviously, one does not want to dull the surface of the metal with sandpaper. A putty knife can be used easily for this job, or if you feel that even this will scratch the metal, put a little piece of rag around the end of the blade.

If the bed has not been painted but is simply black with age and tarnish, the 0000 steel wool and household ammonia will do the job. The super-fine steel wool will not scratch the metal. The ammonia will not give you a shiny finish, only a clean surface. The steel wool will remove the pock marks. After cleaning the bed, then use brass polish to shine it. When the job is complete, the finish should be mirror-like.

IRON FURNITURE

Iron Beds Trimmed with Brass

There are many beds around that are painted iron with brass trim (Fig. 6-3). In most cases, the brass knobs, as well as the iron parts on these beds have been painted. Unless the bed has been outdoors in a junkyard for a long time and is in extremely bad condition, the paint from the iron will not have to be removed—just sanded enough to give a smooth surface to repaint. *Do* remove the paint from the brass trim. This type of

6-3

furniture is extremely adaptable for a modern house or apartment.

Wrought Iron Furniture

Wrought iron furniture can be very decorative for indoor or outdoor use. Do not pass it by if you live in an apartment with no terrace or patio. This type of furniture is found at many garage sales and can be bought very inexpensively most of the time—especially if you find a glass topped table with the glass missing.

If the furniture is to be used inside, there is no need to use a rust-proof base paint, but it is worth the extra effort if the iron furniture is to be used outside, since it will save you from having to repaint for many an extra year.

The glass topped tables are excellent for use in a small dining area because the glass top gives an illusion of more space. A glass top is not a good idea for a low table because people tend to sit on coffee tables, and it is so easy for a small child to fall against one.

Wrought iron furniture is such fun to redo for an apartment because the ideas for refinishing are endless; just choose your color scheme and paint away. Flat paint is usually more suitable than a glossy enamel, and this can be finished with any overtone or antiqued look under the sun.

6-4

It goes without saying that for outdoor use, outdoor paint must be used. If the paint does need to be stripped, follow the same instructions as for wood. Sandpaper may be used on this furniture; since it is going to be repainted, there is no need to worry about scratching the surface.

The copper tub in Figure 6-4 was cleaned in the same way as an unpainted brass bed—ammonia, steel wool, and brass or copper polish. On this type of job as well as on the brass bed, if you have an electric buffer, use it by all means!

7
Mosaics

The use of mosaics for decoration is hardly a new idea. This has been going on for thousands of years. Luckily for everyone who plans to use mosaics, there is no need to go to the nearest quarry and hack out rocks of different colors to make your own tiles in this primitive way.

Webster's gives the following definition of *mosaic:* "the process of making pictures or designs by inlaying small bits of colored stone, glass, etc. in mortar." Consider this definition before you begin, because your project certainly does *not* have to be made of all uniform square ceramic tiles. This would create a rather prosaic mosaic.

You will discover that doing mosaics is fun! When it comes to variety and color, the sky is the limit. The use of mosaics is just about the easiest way in the world to retop a table or chest, making it absolutely weather and waterproof, and alcohol-proof as well. (Figs. 7-1 and 7-2)

7-1

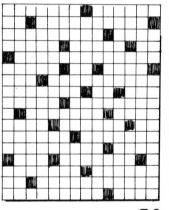

7-2

This chapter is not intended to contain all the detail on mosaics which you would find in a book on the subject. If you find that after trying the various simple examples included in this chapter, you really would like to go in for this art in detail, there are several good books on the subject.

A mosaic design can be made of almost anything—beads, pebbles found on the beach, beach glass (that lovely velvety smooth glass with the colors softened by the sand), bits of broken flowerpots, glass marbles, seeds; almost any bit of glass or clay or stone may be used in a mosaic.

However, for the tabletop which will be discussed here, as unromantic and unimaginative as it sounds, the commercially made uniform ceramic tiles are best. Just because the tiles are commercially made, does not mean that they have to be dull. There are a number of sources for tiles, and the prices will vary according to the source and the type that you choose.

There are the old familiar tiles seen on kitchen counters and bathroom floors, and the choice of color is excellent. The shapes of these tiles do not have to be alike for a smooth surface, but the *thicknesses must be uniform*. No matter how large or how small, if the mosaic top is to be used as a place for bottles, glasses, vases, or any other such articles, the top surface must be as smooth as possible (Figs. 7-3 and 7-4). Your originality and versatility can be demonstrated in your design and in the variety of color and shape of the tiles.

MOSAIC SUPPLIES AND MATERIALS

Assuming that you have an old coffee table, card table, or wrought iron table or bench which could use a new top, the same familiar first rule applies in mosaic tile work as with any other type of refinishing. Decide what you want to do and make a list of the materials needed.

If your project is to be a top for a coffee or dining table, remember that the completed top will be very heavy, and make certain that your base is sturdy enough. If the piece of furniture to be rejuvenated is an old table of questionable wood and condition, your first decision will be whether to paint or to restore it to the natural finish.

Mosaics 63

Since the kind of mosaic work discussed here is for the more casual and informal furniture for use in a playroom, porch, or terrace, paint is probably appropriate for the base. The materials needed for taking down and restoring to a natural finish are listed in Chapter 3 and those for painted furniture are in Chapter 5, so the materials given in this chapter will be only those necessary for the actual tile work. They are as follows:

1. Tiles
2. Sandpaper
3. Tile cement in a tube
4. Grout for filling in the spaces between the tiles
5. Stone chisel
6. Tile nippers
7. Grout and tile cleaner
8. Grout and tile sealer
9. Sponges and rags
10. Coffee cans or large open-mouthed jars (cut the top half off a gallon plastic jug—these are great for mixing grout)

Most of the supplies on the above list can be found at the hardware store; the rest can be found in bathroom supply stores and craft shops, tile manufacturer's shops, or by mail order from dealers who specialize in mosaic tiles and tile equipment. If you happen to live in a small town which has no store selling tiles, they may be ordered from American Handicrafts, 1920 8th

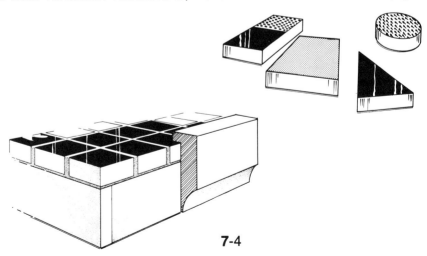

7-3

7-4

Ave., Ft. Worth, TX 76110. This company has stores in almost every state. Write them for a catalog with address nearest you.

There are numerous excellent sources for tiles. When you see the various catalogs, you will discover the many strikingly beautiful Italian glass tiles and immediately envision many uses for them. The handmade glass or glazed tiles are much too expensive for most people to buy in quantity to cover a large surface, but they are beautiful to use for bright clear accents of color. You will find that the prices of tiles vary according to color. A red tile will be quite expensive. Even though technicians have learned to send people to the moon, they still have not learned how to make a truly clear red in ceramics that is inexpensive to produce.

Many, if not all, of the stores from which you can order loose tiles, also will have kits listed in their catalogs. If you choose to do so, there is nothing wrong with using a tile kit. However, there are a number of disadvantages in doing this. One major disadvantage is the lack of originality in the design in a kit. If you buy a kit, even though you may lay the tiles and do all the menial work yourself, you still will not have the complete satisfaction of the result being inimitably your own. You do not have to be an artist to create your own beautiful design. Think what little children do in finger-painting just with the use of color. If the choice is between personality and professionalism, personality wins a blue ribbon every time.

It is true that the design from a kit will be quite handsome. It will be symmetrical and striking, but genuine creativeness has its own style which no one but you can produce. The mosaic kits are hard to resist; and if, on a first try at this type of work, you will feel more comfortable working with a tested pattern, then that is what you should do.

Kits are expensive; generally, they will be at least double the price of the same quantity of loose tiles and other materials needed. With the purchase of the kit, you are not only paying for equipment, you are paying for the privilege of using someone else's design.

Now, back to the list of materials. If there is a ceramic tile shop—the kind that sells just ordinary floor tiles—in your area, you have a veritable gold mine. Nothing could sound less interesting than bathroom and kitchen tiles until you see them for yourself. Today, even bathroom tiles are manufactured in a startling array of colors; solids and spatters, glazed and un-

Mosaics 65

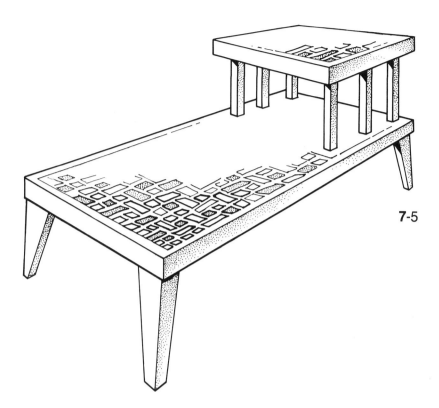

7-5

glazed (I'm partial to the unglazed), and in every conceivable shape. This type of ceramic tile is relatively cheap to buy because it is not made by hand.

Many tile manufacturers and distributors who ordinarily sell only to builders and contractors will sell a few pounds of loose tiles to an individual who wants tile only for a small project such as a tabletop.

One company that manufactures ceramic tile, The American Olean Tile Co. of Pittsburgh, has come up with a new product in tile. It is a unit of four square feet of ceramic tile completely grouted on a rubber backing. This sells for about $1.50 a square foot and may be cut to fit any size, mounted on plywood and used for a tabletop. This company has stores all over the United States.

The list of materials needed and the tiles suggested above complete the necessary ingredients for a mosaic tabletop—with one exception.

Unless the table has a raised edge against which you can butt the outer rows of tiles, you will need some kind of edging (Fig. 7-5). There are a number of different edging materials available. These are discussed at the end of this chapter.

WHERE TO BEGIN

First of all decide on your color scheme. This means the colors for both the frame of the table as well as for the tile top. Either blend or contrast your colors. For example, in re-doing casual porch furniture, a Chinese red frame with blue and white tiles is attractive or a black frame with black and white tile, or varying shades of green for a patio, or try yellows for a game room. Tiles come in such magnificent colors; and there is no problem in having paint mixed to match any color.

When the color scheme has been decided, assemble all the materials needed for the project and get ready to work. Painting the table itself will come first. Sand the table to a smoothness for painting. Remember that you do not have to remove the entire finish. If, however, the old finish happens to be a mahogany stain, a coat of shellac is a good idea before painting. Of all the wood stains, mahogany is the worst for bleeding through new paint. The coat of shellac is a good sealer to prevent bleeding. It goes without saying, do not apply the paint until the shellac has dried completely. Two coats of paint are best for the frame because you want the smoothest possible finish. Any type of enamel may be used for the painting, either flat, semi-gloss, or high gloss. Just be sure to use *enamel*. If the furniture is to be used outdoors, the high gloss paint will stand the elements better, but the flat or satin finish has a dressier appearance for indoor use.

After the paint has dried thoroughly, you may begin work on the mosaic itself. Although it will not be necessary to paint the top of the table since it will be covered with tiles, give the top a coat of shellac for waterproofing before setting the tiles. It will be very hard to resist the temptation to start setting the tiles right away, but while the paint is drying, the tiles can be *soaking*.

PREPARING THE TILES

We are discussing ordinary builders' tiles here. If you buy a mosaic tile kit, follow the directions provided with the kit.

There are two reasons for soaking ceramic tiles in water. One is that these tiles are backed by brown paper which must be removed. Soaking the tiles in a pail of lukewarm water will safely remove the paper. The second reason for soaking is that the grout (used for filling in spaces) is mixed with water, and the tiles will absorb the water from the grout and pop out of place as soon as they are dry if they have not been well soaked with water beforehand.

Any old scrub bucket (if it is clean) will do to soak them. Use lukewarm water, and carefully immerse the tiles completely, covering them for 15 minutes to half an hour. After this, you will find that most of the brown paper has come off and what is left can be taken off very easily. Let the tiles dry on a flat surface covered with absorbent paper (large grocery bags will do for this). Do *not* use newspapers, since the newsprint is likely to come off onto the wet tiles. Then, you would have a real problem on your hands (or on the tiles).

Before permanently setting the dry tiles on your tabletop with adhesive, take a few of the tiles and make two rows, across and down, along the sides of the table. By doing this, you will get a fair idea, not only of the number of tiles needed for the project, but of how well they will fit into the space allotted.

More than likely as you progress around the table, you will discover that a few of the tiles will have to be cut slightly to fit in some of the edges and around the corners of the tabletop. If you have *tile nippers,* cutting is no problem.

Take the nippers in one hand and hold the tile between thumb and forefinger of the other, and "nip" away until the size seems about right. The dimensions of each tile do not have to be exact. If the spacing in some areas seems wider than in others, that is easily filled in later with grout.

If you really want an abstract art mosaic top, break all the tiles with a hammer and *stone chisel* and fit the pieces together like a jigsaw puzzle, combining all the colors. Although this is a much slower way of setting the tiles than doing them whole, the effect is unusual and attractive when completed—and definitely original.

If you want a specific picture or design with your tiles, sketch the design in pencil on the table top itself, and using the *tile adhesive,* first set the tiles in the design you have drawn, and work out from there.

After the tiles have been set in place with the adhesive, mix the grout. A coffee can is perfect for this. Put about half a cup of *dry grout* into the coffee can and add water until the grout has the consistency of thin oatmeal or library paste. The grout in the can dries quickly, almost like plaster of paris, so do not mix too much at one time. The grout does not all have to be applied in one operation, so take your time. Don't feel that the entire tabletop has to be finished in one evening.

Find either a *putty knife* or a *rubber kitchen spatula* and begin to spread the grout over the tiles, making sure that all the spaces between the tiles are filled. Using a knife or spatula is the "scientific" way of spreading grout, though you will probably end up using your fingers. Spreading the grout is an art in itself. It is far better to spread many thin coats rather than to try to put on one thick coat.

After spreading the grout and making sure that all cracks are filled, take a clean damp cloth or sponge and wipe off excess grout. Wipe not only the tiles but around the frame of the table as well. Let the tiles dry thoroughly for a few days and wipe again with a clean damp rag.

The final step in the work is to apply some kind of sealer, since tiles, particularly unglazed tiles, are quite porous—as is the grout. *Varnish* is a very good sealer. Use either the glossy or satin finish, and simply spread the varnish on with a paintbrush.

There is a special *silicone sealer* made just for mosaic work, but it can be bought only in craft shops. If there is a craft shop in your area, buy the silicone sealer. It is not expensive. If there is no such shop nearby, buy the varnish. Either one is fine.

EDGING

If your tiles were set down *into* a tabletop, your work is finished. But, if the tiles were set *on top* of the piece of wood, you will need some kind of edging (Fig. 7-6). This edging can be put on before tiling or after. Doing the edging *first* is better if you are using wood molding because your tile work will be smoother, but if you are using some other edging, it is better to do it last.

If your molding is of wood, it can be whatever depth you choose. Rather than wood, some people find an anodized aluminum molding more satisfactory because it comes in several finishes such as brass, copper, or aluminum and can be

Refinished pine and poplar (doors) dry sink with set in repair on "splash" board.

Unfinished pine box.

One hour later, refinished pine box using Rub n' Buff.

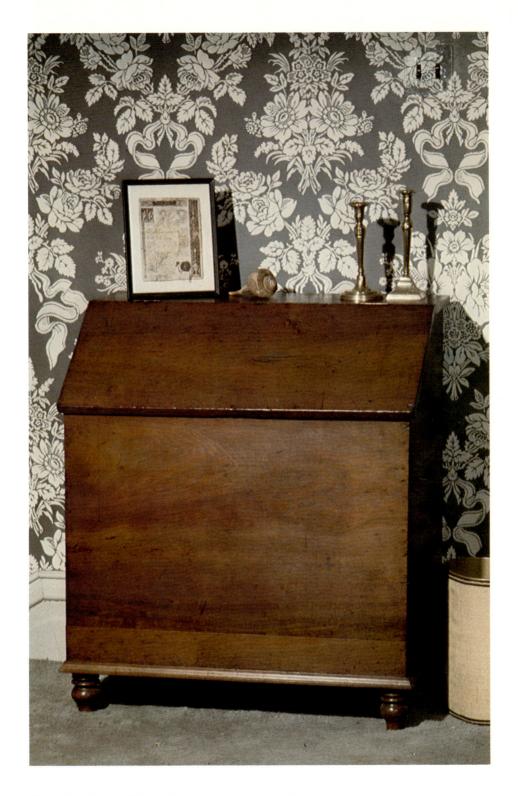

Walnut feed bin refinished by wax-shellac method; now being used for storage.

*Italian antique bentwood rocker.
Instead of refinishing in a natural state,
the frame was sprayed with Wet Paint
and the cane brush was painted with flat enamel.*

Various brasses that have been cleaned and polished and sprayed with Boat Nu (from top to bottom) drawer pulls; Chinese lock; Chinese lock plate; bolt cover from four poster bed; key hole cover and bottom; drawer pull.

top:
Dime store metal wastebaskets covered in fabric: left, trimmed in braid with cross-stitched monogram; right, covered with burlap and decorated with felt and sequins.

bottom:
Dime store metal wastebaskets: left, covered with Con-Tact and ruffles bought at a fabric store; right, covered with wallpaper and trimmed with braid from the fabric store.

Pine foot stool (99¢ at the variety store) done in decoupage with designs cut from gift wrapping paper.

Copper wash tub which was cleaned professionally. This does not have to be done professionally, but since I paid practically nothing for it in its original state, it seemed worthwhile to have it cleaned by a professional. See Fig. 6-4 for wash tub before cleaning.

Maple rocker refinished by the wax-shellac method.
Each type of wood treated this way retains its own character.

Department store maple hutch which has been antiqued without painted decoration.

Small book case which originally was unpainted furniture. Painted with Old Colonial paint; porcelain knobs from the hardware sto[re]

attached to the edge of the wood base with *screws*. The screws are bought with the molding. *Do not use nails or brads*. Either one of these will fall out after a while. The molding must be absolutely tight—without bulges. You can do this yourself, but most picture framers or lumberyards that carry the molding will do it for you for a dollar or two.

There is also a type of plastic molding available in a variety of simulated metals and woods, but it is not recommended—either here in this book or by most mosaic craftsmen.

When starting to set the tiles on a tabletop bound by molding, begin at the very edge, so that the smallest possible area will be left for filling in the grout. You will then continue setting the tiles as previously discussed. Remember when the molding is used, it will come *above* the surface of the tabletop. The object of the molding is to cover the sides of the tiles.

Some people prefer painted grout. This is certainly a matter of personal choice. If you think that you would like the grout colored, you may do one of two things. While mixing the grout, mix the pigment with a special paint for this which may be bought in any craft shop. The other way to color grout, which is a little bit more painstaking than the first, is to take oil paints and a small watercolor or oil paintbrush and paint the grout only in certain sections of the mosaic.

If you have made a particular design with your tiles, sometimes a bit of gold paint for accent can be good. You can either blend or contrast the colors of the grout with the colors of the tiles. This paint is added *after* the grout is completely dry. Any painting of the grout must be done before covering the tiles with the sealer.

USING ANTIQUE TILES

If you are fortunate enough to have found antique tiles in a shop somewhere, it is better *not* to use these for a tabletop. Old tiles are likely to be brittle and crack easily. A favorite use for antique tiles, even if you own only a few, is to place them around a fireplace facing. If your fireplace has unattractive brick facing, redoing it and setting in tiles is not a particularly difficult task.

First, the tiles must be perfectly clean and free, not only of

7-7

old mortar, but of any grease and dirt. Once the tiles are clean, the other steps are as follows:

1. Use a knife or very coarse sandpaper to scar the backs of the tiles.

2. Put a thin coat of cement over the entire brick facing of the fireplace. Use pre-mixed prepared concrete; there are many brands available, but be sure to use a *sand* mix rather than one of the heavier mixes. Follow the directions on the package, and after applying the mixture to the fireplace, allow to dry for 24 hours.

3. After the base cement is thoroughly dry, apply a thin coat (1/4 to 1/2" of fresh cement to your base. Press the tiles in this. Use a thin trowel to fill in and smooth around the tiles. Wipe off excess amount.

Figure 7-7 illustrates the principle of covering the brick facing with cement and then setting the tiles.

If you do not have a fireplace, or if you rent your house and do not want to leave the tiles there permanently, then make a wall hanging. Take two or three of the tiles (depending on the size) and with epoxy glue attach them to a board which has been painted in a color to blend or contrast with the tiles. Plywood is excellent for this. Then choose an appropriate picture frame molding to put around the board and hang your tile picture on the wall. This way, you can take the tiles with you when you move.

8
Picture Frames

During the early 1960s, two Englishmen, Michael Flanders and Donald Swann, appeared in a popular Broadway show, "At the Drop of a Hat." One of its hit songs was "It's Terribly House and Garden"—which is terribly appropriate today for as serious a book on furniture refinishing as this one. No one knows better than the people who go in for refinishing exactly to what extremes all those *other* people go to be so "terribly house and garden." However, in spite of Flanders and Swann, one does not have to be un-chic just because there are a few pictures and mirrors hanging about—or they would be hanging about if they were not in such dire need of refinishing!

There are about a half dozen really superior reasons for refinishing frames for pictures or mirrors. If you are going in for antiques, frames are relatively plentiful and cheap. If you are a novice at refinishing, re-doing a frame is hardly a life-time project. When one can see good results in such a short period of

Picture Frames 73

time, it is encouraging to have the confidence to go on to bigger, though not necessarily better, things.

Nine times out of ten, accessories for the home are a good place for the beginner to start his refinishing. Sometimes—there is always that tenth time—an intricate but badly nicked or chipped gold leaf frame can cause more trouble in refinishing than a large, plainer piece of furniture.

Some of the more common frames to be found now are the Victorian frames, both large and small, of gold leaf in various stages of ornamentation and disrepair. They have the leaf over wood or plaster or sometimes both, depending on the ornateness of the frame. If you have been lucky enough to find an old plaster frame, then no matter what it looks like now, there is no real problem in refinishing. Ignore your spouse's comments when you bring it in the house.

The majority of all the old gold-leaf frames are gold leaf over plaster of paris over wood. All embellishments are of plaster. Sometimes this plaster is solid; and at other times, it serves only to cover a lovely plain pine or walnut frame. For the moment, the frame to be considered for restoration will be the plaster and leaf (Fig. 8-1).

8-1

MATERIALS FOR REFINISHING

The materials needed for the restoration are neither exotic nor hard to come by. They may all be bought at the hardware store and are as follows:

1. Small bag of plaster of paris (if your hardware store does not have this, every drug store does)
2. Very, very fine sandpaper
3. Water color brushes
4. A 1" paintbrush
5. Bronzing liquid or Rub 'n Buff leaf (bronzing liquid is a product which is similar to banana oil and is used in the mixing of the leaf powder)
6. BB shot—this just happens to be the same size as nearly all beading found on this kind of gold leaf frame
7. Pumice powder—can also be found at the drug store
8. Mild soap, rags, and the good old scrub bucket.

RESTORING THE FRAME

8-2

Once you have acquired all the necessary materials for restoring your gold leaf frame, you are ready to work. As always, the first requirement in refinishing anything is soap and water; so clean the frame well, get the dust and grease out of all those corners, and let dry thoroughly.

After a careful scrutiny of the extent and nature of any damage of the carefully cleaned plaster frame (Fig. 8-2), the next step is to repair the broken plaster. Replacing nicked or lost beading is delicate restorative work, but fun.

If you have never worked with plaster of paris before, it is well to keep in mind these three important facts: (1) a little bit goes a long long way; (2) it dries and hardens almost before you have time to turn around; (3) mix only very small amounts, one or two tablespoons, at a time with water until it has thickened to the consistency of putty.

When preparing the plaster, mix only what will be used at one time; once the water is added, the plaster cannot be put away for future use. Once it has hardened, it cannot be re-used no matter how much hot water you try to add. Get out a coffee can or your cut-off plastic jug; you just cannot beat these for throw-away mixing bowls.

Before adding the water to the plaster, take a ruler and measure the damaged sections of beading on the frame. Each section is repaired individually. The new beading is not made in one long strip to be cut later. Measure both the length and width of the broken sections of your frame, writing down the dimensions of each. Then, as with clay, take the plaster of paris which you have mixed with water and mold a similar size strip to the original beading.

Then, using an ordinary sharp-pointed paring knife, trim the plaster molding to *almost* exact size. While the plaster is still quite damp and malleable, take the BB's and place each one in the plaster molding the proper distance apart to match the original molding in the frame. Now the plaster looks like a finger with BB's in it (Fig. 8-3)! What could be easier than that?

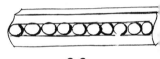

8-3

By this time, approximately five minutes should have passed, and the rough piece of beading has begun to harden enough to handle. Take the new section and place it in the frame in the space to be replaced. No glue is needed for this. The damp plaster will secure it in the frame.

Finally, taking a little of the remaining plaster from the coffee can, lightly cover the BB's that were used in the molding. Take the old paring knife again, and, if necessary, trim the new molding down to size to match the old. Let this harden overnight before attempting to cover it with gold leaf.

If there is more than one section of beading to be done, and there usually is, do the other sections in the same manner. If your picture frame has elaborate molding to be repaired other than beading, simply mix your plaster of paris in the same proportions. Mold the leaves, ropes, or other decorations and apply them to the frame in the same way.

If there is a large hardware store or lumberyard in your area that carries a good supply of wooden picture frame moldings, it will not be necessary to go through the process of making your own beading. Simply buy a strip of wooden beading the same size as that which you are trying to repair. Glue it on and cover with gold leaf.

8-4

8-5

REGILDING THE PLASTER

Gold enamel paint is *not* used to regild a gold leaf frame. The enamel gives a garish look (the kind you see on radiators in the ladies' rooms in hospitals and bus stations). Bronzing powder combined with banana oil or bronzing liquid is the best mixture for regilding. This is what you use if you plan to mix your own.

Take a small china or glass bowl and put in several tablespoons of bronzing powder; add the banana oil, a few drops at a time, and mix well. When this mixture is the consistency of paint, it is ready to apply. Use a water-color brush or a 1/2" paintbrush, depending on the size of the frame.

When you go to buy the bronzing powder, you will be surprised to see how many different shades of gold there are. Be sure that you choose a shade that will blend well with the rest of the room in which the frame will be used, particularly if there are other gold frames. There is no such thing as just "plain gold."

If the frame which you are re-gilding is not huge, once again the product to use is Rub 'n Buff (Fig. 8-4). They have a number of different shades of gilt. Just follow the directions on the tube, but for a larger frame, this can become expensive.

WOOD VENEER FRAMES

Everyone is familiar with the large, wide, dark wood veneer frames which were popular at the turn of the century (Fig. 8-5). The veneer on top was usually stained a very dark, almost black color, and by 1974 this stain has reached the old familiar alligator look with the checking that occurs so often. What in the world can be done to redeem this frame?

There are several choices. You may paint the frame (see Chapter 5), or you may restore the frame to its natural finish. If you will re-read Chapters 3 and 4 of this book, you will find all the necessary instructions for restoration to a natural finish. But, before *any* refinishing can be started, something must be done about the old finish. With this particular type of frame, there is a very special and very easy way to remove the old finish—*sans* sanding, *sans* paint and varnish, and minus lye, too!

Clean, warm water is the answer! Take your frame and soak it in a laundry tub or even in the bathtub if you do not mind foregoing a bath for a night or two or three. Be sure that the *whole* frame is completely immersed at one time. This is all you have to do. Leave the frame in the water for several days. Actually, it will not do a bit of harm to the frame to be out of the water for a while if you want to use the tub—just be sure you put it back in the bath when you are through.

Check on the frame once or twice during this soaking period, and if you think that the veneer is not loosening fast enough, add a little warm water to the tub. This will help dissolve the glue that is holding the veneer. Do not add hot water, thinking this might hasten the process. Hot water will hasten only the spoilage of the good wood beneath the veneer.

After a few days in the tub, the outer layer of veneer will peel right off the solid wood; and underneath you will find a perfectly lovely wood frame, probably of pine. It could be oak if you are not so lucky.

This solid pine frame that remains after all veneer and glue have been removed will have to have a good long period of drying time (at least a week) before any refinishing can be attempted.

You may certainly refinish your frame in any way you choose—either naturally using the shellac and wax method as mentioned in Chapter 4 or by using a stain of some sort if you do not care for the color of the original wood.

There are a number of finishes on the market, but there is one in particular that gives walnut the most beautiful rich brown color, emphasizing all the grain. This is simply called Oil Finish®, but this brand can be bought only from the Door Stores, Inc. Many antique dealers, however, sell this same kind of oil finish, and Min-Wax now has an oil finish which is a very good stain. If the solid wood of the frame turns out to be some undesirable color after the veneer is removed, simply stain it or paint it any shade or color that you wish.

Brown paste shoe polish is a wonderful finish for a picture frame. Usually one coat of polish is enough, but you can use as many as needed to get as dark a finish as you want.

Finally, no matter what stain you use, if any, except for shoe polish, finish the frame in the good old shellac and wax way. Seven coats are not necessary at all in finishing a picture frame, since a frame does not get the hard day to day wear and tear of a chest or table. You will need only to shellac and wax once or twice. This is enough for a good finish.

USING PLASTER AND GOLD LEAF OVER SOLID WOOD

In Victorian times, there were more ingenious methods for covering perfectly beautiful solid wood than veneer. A favorite type of frame of the same era as solid plaster was the plaster and gold over wood (Fig. 8-6). They are not hard to identify because if they are in need of repair at all, you will be able to see the solid wood underneath the plaster.

Usually, the objective of restoration of this type of frame is *not* to repair the plaster. Of course, this depends entirely on

8-6

the condition of the plaster and gold leaf. The point, generally, is to remove the plaster and refinish the wood. And you remove the plaster in the same way that you remove the veneer—by soaking in warm water.

To loosen the plaster before soaking, tap gently with a hammer and peel off what chips you can before soaking. After the plaster has been removed, finish the wood in the same way as after removing veneer. It just depends on what you find underneath all that broken plaster.

UNPAINTED FRAMES

In craft shops, unpainted furniture stores, hardware stores, and variety stores—almost anywhere—you can find every kind of new "do-it-yourself" type of frame for picture or mirror. Many are excellent reproductions of antiques; others are simply ordinary until you add your special finishing touch.

There is no rule or limit as to the best way to refinish these frames. The way that will suit you and the room in which it is to be used is always the best way. Use combinations of gold leaf for inner molding and paint on the outer molding. Use wood stain and the wax-shellac finish. Spray paint to match wallpaper or slip-covers or to pick up a particular color in the picture to be framed.

Shadow frames can be particularly attractive for collections of dried flowers, political campaign buttons, or antique tiles mentioned in Chapter 7. The same advantage goes for new unfinished frames as for the furniture mentioned earlier. Unless you are determined to have an antique, with the use of this type of accessory, there is no stripping or soaking or repairing. Put it together and finish it any way that your heart desires.

9
Trays, Wastebaskets and Small Furniture

DECORATING TRAYS AND WASTEBASKETS

Most people who plan to decorate a tray or wastebasket already have several around the house that are nicked, rusted, stained, or simply have the design worn off from daily wear and tear. However, there are others who plan to buy a new tray or basket just for the purpose of decoration to go in a certain room. Some are lucky enough to have acquired an antique tole tray.

Just in case there is some question in your mind about "tole," it is nothing more than a French word for sheet metal. According to Patricia Nimocks' book *Decoupage* (Scribner, $9.95), various articles were made of tole or tin to copy the more expensive porcelains made in earlier times.

If you are one of the rare creatures who owns an original

82 Furniture Refinishing at Home

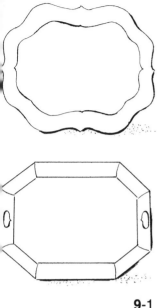

9-1

Chippendale or Revere tray (Fig. 9-1), and if the original tray is in anywhere near half decent condition, do *not* try to refinish it. Doing this will spoil its antique value. If the tray is really horrible, do give refinishing a try because if the tray is that rusty and worn, the antique value is not that great in the first place.

The best thing to do is to buy a new tray or basket. The dime store is a good source of supply, and hardware stores or craft shops sometimes carry trays or wastebaskets to be used just for the purpose of decoration. Even if these baskets have a painted decoration on them, they can be sanded to a smooth finish in a few minutes and covered with spray paint.

Decoupage

Appliquéing prints on trays is one of the easiest ways of decorating. If you are interested in antiques, old prints, or new prints which you make look old, are perfect for this purpose.

Old or new, choose the print according to the size of the tray and according to your own hobby, profession or taste. Book jackets make excellent decorations, as well as newspaper articles of particular importance—not only family wedding or engagement announcements, but elections, coronations, trips into space, and the like are good for this purpose.

If you have a new print that you wish were old, there is no need for wishful thinking because with the twist of a tea bag the print can be as old as you like. Make a dish of strong tea and soak the picture in it. Completely immerse the print in the tea until it is stained a light brown (Fig. 9-2). When the print has partially dried—enough to handle—but is still damp, gently fray its edges. With the stain of the tea and the frayed edges, you will have as authentic looking an "old" print as any around, and for much less cost. After tearing the edges of the print, let it dry completely before trying to glue it on the tray or basket.

Materials Needed
1. Metal tray or wastebasket (the tray can certainly be of wood; you are not likely to have a wooden waste basket)
2. Suitable prints of any size (old or new)
3. Fine sandpaper

Trays, Wastebaskets and Small Furniture **83**

4. Spray paint
5. Linseed oil
6. Turpentine
7. Gold enamel
8. Masking tape
9. Varnish (satin finish or glossy)
10. Tea
11. Watercolor brushes
12. Pencil and ruler
13. Scissors (good and sharp)
14. Casein glue
15. Raw Turkey umber

Preparation of the Tray or Wastebasket If the tray you bought has a painted design which you do not like, apply a little paint remover to the design itself. When the remover begins to blister, take off remover and design with a putty knife. When this has dried, take the finest grade of sandpaper and make the surface of the tray as smooth as possible. Now, spray the entire tray in any color you wish.

When the paint has dried, take a pencil and ruler and

9-2

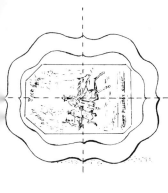

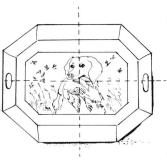

9-3

mark on the tray the exact spot where the print should go (Fig. 9-3). If you do not measure first, you will smear glue all over the newly painted tray when the time comes to paste on the picture. Measure first to avoid having the print slide around after the paste is on the back.

When the print has been glued in place on the tray or basket, let it dry thoroughly. You may leave the tray as it is with no further trim, or you may edge the print and handles of the tray with a gold border. To do this edging, use gold enamel and a watercolor brush. You may even want an overtone if the base color of your tray has been a pastel. The recipe for the overtone is as follows:

2 tablespoons raw (burnt) Turkey umber
3 tablespoons turpentine
1 tablespoon clear waterproof varnish
A drop or two of linseed oil (to keep it from drying too fast)

Appliquéing the Print
1. Apply mixture with a paintbrush.
2. Wad soft clean cloth and rub off overtone with a circular motion.
3. Leave darker tones in corners and joinings of tray.
4. Have center of tray much lighter.
5. Coat with varnish after overtone is completely dry.

The above is basically the same formula that is used on furniture. However, in antiquing a tray or any small item, you will wipe off more of the overtone than you would on a piece of furniture. Otherwise, your tray will seem to be all overtone and no picture.

Several coats of varnish are necessary for a tray, since here again, as well as with a tabletop, you have an article to hold dishes and glasses and other things which are likely to leave rings.

A final word on appliquéing prints. You certainly are not obligated to use an entire picture on the tray. Sometimes the background of the tray itself will be more effective than the background of the picture, so very neatly and carefully cut only the actual design which you want to use from the whole print (Figs. 9-4, 9-5, and 9-6).

9-4

9-5

9-6

86   Furniture Refinishing at Home

9-8

9-7

Painting with a Design or Stencil

If you are going in for the "antique" look, the tray or wastebasket should have a dull rather than a glossy finish to begin with (Fig. 9-7). If you prefer the "modern" look, there are some fantastic super glossy paints called *wet paint* which come in every wild color imaginable. Whichever look you choose, the directions are the same. Spray the tray or wastebasket for the smoothest possible finish. Artists' oils and red sable brushes are used for the painting of the actual design. Use short-stemmed brushes, since the long stems are too hard to handle for such precise delicate work (Fig. 9-8). Use the brushes as though you were drawing with a pencil.

For ease of explanation here, we will discuss decorating a tray. However, if it is a wastebasket you plan to decorate with paint, the process is basically the same as for trays.

If the wastebasket will take a lot of abuse, such as in a den, a coat of varnish will protect your design and allow you to dust without removing the overtone. If the wastebasket will get little use, such as in a guest room, a coat of wax will give enough protection.

Materials Needed
1. Artists' oil paints in colors of your choice (small tubes)
2. Red sable long-hair oil brushes in sizes #1 or #2 and #5 or #6; be sure these brushes have short stems
3. Fibre-seal® (available at craft shops or art supply stores)—this is the medium with which you will mix your paint; do not use turpentine
4. Small paper cup for holding medium
5. Disposable aluminum tray; this is your palette
6. Wax or varnish

A disposable aluminum tray will make a fine inexpensive pallette for your oils. Arrange your colors in small amounts around the palette with the small paper cup (or an old shot glass) for holding the medium, which in this case if Fibre-seal placed at the end of the pallette.

Planning and Transferring the Design The first step in painting your tray is to plan your design. The design must be in proportion to the size of the tray. You would not use a small bouquet of forget-me-nots on a 2 foot by 1 foot Revere tray.

Your design may come from any source whatsoever as long as the design fits within the bounds of the tray. If you have trouble drawing or finding your own design, you may want to use a stencil. If you are using a stencil, you will not have to trace the design; simply tape the stencil to the tray and paint. (See "Finishing.")

If the design is taken from a magazine or from any source which is not your own, it may be traced using any reasonable transparent paper; onionskin is very good for this. There are many excellent books which contain designs for painting trays as well as furniture. "American Home Crafts" magazine has patterns for painted furniture, which, of course, can be applied to trays as well; The American Handicrafts Co. also has pattern books for painted designs.

After the design has been traced onto the transparent paper, it then must be transferred to the surface of the tray. This is done with the use of artists' tracing paper, which is a heavy carbon paper. The carbon paper which you can buy in sewing departments for use with dress patterns is very good to use because it comes in several colors. If your tray is black, buy white tracing paper; if your tray is light, obviously, you want dark tracing paper.

Use cellophane tape to attach the tracing paper to the tray, and tape the design to the tracing paper. If the paper or design moves during the process of tracing, you've had it! There is no way that you will be able to get the paper back to just the right spot again. Use a hard lead pencil with a good sharp point for transferring the design to the tray with the tracing paper. After the design has been transferred successfully to the tray, remove the tracing paper.

Finishing You are now ready to paint. Fill in the design on the tray with a light "wash." This wash will be a combination of white artists' oil paint thinned with a product called Fibre-seal. Fibre-seal is fast drying. The purpose of this wash is to glaze the design. Allow the glaze to dry completely.

The next step is to fill in the pattern with artists' oil paints in the colors desired. When filling in, *work with one color at a time;* when you have finished with one color, and it has dried completely, you may introduce the next color. When filling in your colors on a leaf or similar shaped design always work toward a point (Fig. 9-9). Overnight drying is recommended.

After all basic colors have been applied, you next work with tones or highlights. All this means is that you are adding depth to your design. When your tones or highlights have dried thoroughly (which again means overnight), any leaves in your design are to be veined; this is the final step and needs the greatest care of all. To end a point in your design, lift the brush; otherwise the design will smear. For a clear outline of the design, when the picture is almost but not quite dry, take a Q-tip® and thinner and the Fibre-seal and go around the edges of the design. Let your tray dry for *one week.*

When the paint is completely dry, it must have a protective coat of some sort, and the whole tray must be coated with one or two coats of varnish, either glossy or dull, as you choose.

Hints This kind of painted design on a tray is not difficult, but it is precise, careful, delicate work. It takes a great deal of time; and if you are impatient by nature, do not attempt such designs on trays.

Although the rule is not to refinish antique tole trays in half-way decent condition (this would be like redoing original painted decorations on an authentic Pennsylvania Dutch chest), there certainly are many trays in such rusty and battered condition that no trace of the design is visible. If you have one of these, then go right ahead and do anything you can to revive it.

Naturally, the surface will have to be washed to remove any oil or grease and then sanded to take a new coat of paint. There are many good rust removers on the shelf at the supermarket or hardware store. If the rust is not too bad, a little sanding will take care of it. If the original background paint has worn through to the bare tin, use a metal primer paint before spraying with the final color. Otherwise, you will find that within a very short while, the paint will start to peel, and then you will be right back where you started.

After completing the background painting of your tray and letting it dry well, then choose your design, staying as much in character as possible with the original. This may be done either with paint or decoupage.

Using Decorative Fabrics

A simple wastebasket can easily become one of the most decorative objects in a room. With a wastebasket you are not

9-10

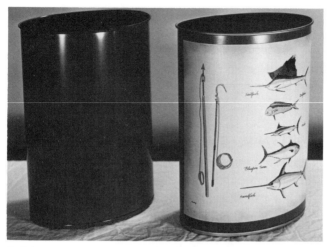

9-11

9-12

limited to paint or decoupage for decoration since nothing that could be harmful is going to be placed on the design.

A marvelous source for wastebasket decoration is the local fabric shop. If you have curtains or spreads made for a bedroom, buy an extra yard of material, cut out the designs and use them for appliques. There are innumerable designs with braids, pleats, ruffles, and ribbons that can be bought for less than a dollar and used as trim around the top or bottom of the basket. Burlap with an embroidered design also makes a good cover, and some people even use velvet with ribbon trim (Fig. 9-10). Felt also is an excellent decorative fabric.

One of the easiest ways to rejuvenate an old metal basket is to cover it with either wallpaper or Con-Tact® and trim the top

Trays, Wastebaskets and Small Furniture 91

and bottom with decorative braid (Fig. 9-11). Dried flowers may be used if they are flat enough and are covered with thin plastic so that they will be protected from being knocked off when dusting or having the family dog chew them off (Fig. 9-12).

People have been decorating baskets and trays for years with the use of wedding invitations. A handsome monogram is always a good idea. The sky is really the limit for this kind of project.

USING DECOUPAGE ON SMALL FURNITURE

Decoupage is a superb way to turn an ordinary unpainted piece of small furniture into a real treasure. The footstool shown in the color section is a good example. This is an ordinary pine stool (cost $1 at the variety store) transformed into a real conversation piece. Decoupage comes from the French word *decouper* which simply means to cut.

My own definition of decoupage is the art of painting with paper and scissors. This means that the most important tool you need for this work is a good pair of sharp, pointed scissors.

There are several books on decoupage; this can become a complicated art form. As previously mentioned, one particularly good book is *Decoupage* by Patricia Nimocks. For simple projects, however, every craft shop has instructional booklets and every type of material needed to do this kind of decoration. The equipment needed is very simple:

1. Sharp scissors and razors
2. Elmer's glue
3. Fine sandpaper
4. Sealer
5. Varnish (made especially for use in decoupage)

It is best to buy these supplies in a craft or hobby shop since the varnishes and sealers are made specifically for decoupage.

There are thousands of prints available that can be bought just for decoupage. However, some of the most attractive designs for this art can be found in left over wallpaper—if you are doing a wastebasket or table for a particular room. Greeting cards and gift wrapping paper are an excellent source of supply. Wedding or graduation invitations can be used; and at the rate that history is being made every day, newspapers are great sources for decoration.

The following decoupage procedure is for furniture that is to be painted before applying decoupage.

1. Sand to a satin finish.
2. Paint object in color of your choice using flat enamel.
3. Using decoupage "sealer," seal your picture *before* cutting. (If you try to spray tiny pieces of paper with sealer, they will fly all over the room.) The purpose of the sealer is to keep any colors or ink in the print from bleeding through the varnish.
4. After the paint has dried, map out the design which you have cut from the print; using Elmer's glue, apply it to the object. Carefully remove any excess glue and let dry *thoroughly*.
5. Now apply several coats of decoupage varnish. Some people use as few as three coats of varnish over the paint; others use as many as ten or twenty. No matter how many coats of varnish you use, you must allow 24 hours drying time between coats. The object in covering the paint is to protect the color. Otherwise, when you start sanding, you would sand away all the color. Do not sand at all until you have built up several coats of varnish. (There are several one-coat decoupage finishes available. They dry to a hard, glossy finish and don't require any sanding.)
6. In sanding, many people prefer to use steel wool of the finest grade rather than sandpaper. I feel that this gives a more satiny surface; if you use the steel wool, though, you must be extremely careful to wipe off any small traces of the metal that invariably shed during the sanding.
7. After the final sanding is completed, finish the top with a spar varnish for protection. This is the type of varnish used on basketball courts and is much tougher than the type usually sold for use in decoupage work. Choose a flat finish rather than glossy.

Twenty coats of varnish are not required on every bit of

decoupage. The amount of use that the piece will get will determine the number of coats of varnish required. Obviously, the foot stool pictured in the color section would require a harder finish than a dresser front or screen which would not have feet or glasses placed on it.

Since there is such a long waiting period between varnishing and sanding, why not work on two projects at once, starting one a day or two ahead of the other. Then, you will have accomplished twice as much in the same length of time.

10
Lamps and Other Accessories

There are all types of people on this planet. There are some who make planters out of lamps, and there are some who make lamps out of planters, and there are others who do actually use lamps for lighting the house. At the present time, though, this last breed mentioned seems to be dying out rapidly. However, all three types will be discussed here (Fig. 10-1).

RESTORING OLD LAMPS

The very attractive planter illustrated in Figure 10-2 was at one time a "gross", to use the teen-age vernacular, hanging light fixture circa 1923 boarding house. To transform this lamp into a useful and decorative planter was perfectly simple, and the materials needed were as follows:

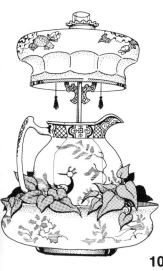

10-1

10-2

10-3

1. Very fine sandpaper
2. Spray paint in your choice of color
3. New chain (much easier and not much more expensive than trying to brighten up the old one)
4. Liner (not used in this case, but a matter of choice; sphagnum moss was used to line this planter)

The first step in the rejuvenation of the light fixture is to remove the antiquated frosted bowl. Throw it away! Sand any old paint until the surface is smooth and clean enough to spray with new paint. Next, spray paint and let dry. Attach your new chain with rings of "S" hooks at the same places as the old chain, and add your plant (Fig. 10-3). If you use artificial greenery, naturally, you will not need a liner. If you use moss with real plants, no liner is needed; unless moss is used for a planter as open as this one, you will need some kind of liner. The type of liner will depend entirely on the room in which the planter is to be hung. If you want only the outline of the planter itself to show, use a heavy clear plastic for lining; sheet copper or even heavy duty aluminum foil may be used as well. Just cut whatever the material is to the proper size, and fit it smoothly inside the planter, so that no rough edges are hanging over.

If you happen to like planter lamps, they are not difficult to make. The most popular lamps of this type, at least the kind you seem to see most often in the department stores, are the "pitcher and washbowl" lamp and the "coffee grinder" lamp with plants shown spilling out of the coffee drawer (Fig. 10-4). The stem of the lamp, the part that contains all the wiring, comes through the pitcher, which is set in the middle of the planter bowl.

If you have found a suitable pitcher and bowl to make your own lamp, do not try to do the wiring yourself. Take it to an electrician for the wiring (even he will not guarantee drilling without breaking) and then bring it home for the planting.

10-4

If you do not want to take the chance of having holes drilled, particularly if your lamp is china or glass and you don't want it broken, I recommend a separate stand or base. Most stores that make or sell lamps carry wooden or metal bases in square, oval, and round shapes. These bases have their stems positioned at the back so that you simply set your lamp on the base and the wiring will be hidden behind it.

There are many interesting old oil lamps in the junk shops and antique stores. Many of them, particularly the metal ones, are not very expensive (especially if there is rust or corrosion to be removed).

Great numbers of nickel-coated brass oil lamps were produced in the late 1880's. Nickel probably was as popular in those days as brass is now. These lamps can be bought very cheaply because most people do not realize that the nickel finish can be removed, leaving a handsome brass lamp.

The removal of a nickel finish is *not* for the "do it yourselfer" because the acid that must be used is far too dangerous to have in the home. Almost any lampmaker will remove this nickel for you, and then you may either buy the proper size harp and fixture for the light or have it wired by an electrician or at the hardware store (Figs. 10-5).

The main disadvantage in wiring the lamp yourself is that in order to keep the cord out of sight, a hole must be drilled

Lamps and Other Accessories **97**

through the lamp; and it is next to impossible to drill a hole in metal without the proper tools. Even by taking your "find" from the junk shop to the lampmaker, you will still be paying less than half of what a new lamp of comparable quality and size would cost; and this way you have just what you want.

There is no need to be obligated to have the nickel removed from your lamp if it is in good condition. In fact, the nickel lamps are a little more unusual.

MAKING WOODEN LAMPS

Your local lumberyard can offer you an endless supply of lamps of any description for very little money. Decide on the kind of lamp you need and make it yourself. A piece of wood 4" x 4" or 6" -6" around is probably the most versatile size to use. Naturally, a lamp of this thickness should be fairly tall, at least 12" of height for the 4" x 4". Choose two more squares of wood in graduating sizes to form a step base (Fig. 10-6).

10-5

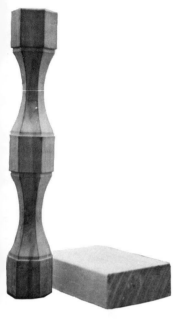

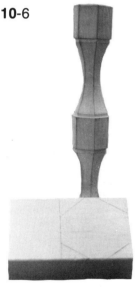

10-6

In order to attach the light fixture, you will need either to glue a small circle of wood to the top of your lamp to which you will attach the light fixture, or if it is the kind of electric fixture that "sets in," carve a circle in the top of the wood and set the fixture in with epoxy.

Refinish your wood in any way that you like before gluing all the pieces together. This will give the completed lamp a smoother look (Fig. 10-7). These lamps may be finished naturally using stain and the wax-shellac method. They are ideal for decoupage.

If you prefer a base that is more elaborate than the simple square, buy small moldings to use for trim. If your requirements are for a dressier lamp, turned table legs or bedposts can be used. Although these are not found in the lumberyard, old wooden candlesticks are excellent for lamps, especially if you come across an odd one in a shop—and the price will probably be very reasonable.

The electric part of the lamp is the easiest of all. Practically every variety store, and certainly every electrical supply store, carries the bulb base and harp that is either "stuck in" or "attached to" your base as mentioned earlier. When you have finished, you will end up with a lamp that looks like 50¢ and only cost you $50! No, that really is not the truth. Give it a try, and it will be such a success that you will end up making lamps that you don't even have a tabletop for.

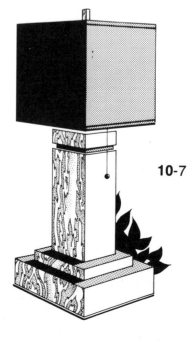

10-7

11
Chairs

WICKER

Wicker furniture is back in style! The old porch and sun room furniture of the twenties and thirties and earlier is moving into the living room with a new look (Fig. 11-1). Wicker is the easiest of the three main types of "grass" or "reed" furniture to rejuvenate.

11-1

If your wicker is split in spots, use an epoxy glue and clamps to repair it. If the wicker is breaking away from its frame, small brads or nails can be used without danger of splitting the wicker or being unsightly. If a piece of wicker is obviously missing, a small piece of thin dowel can be nailed or glued in its place.

The easiest way to paint wicker is with a spray paint, spraying over and under, in front and behind. It is next to impossible to reach every little corner and crack of wicker with a brush. A shiny enamel or one of the new "wet look" paints are much more effective on wicker than a flat paint.

After the chair has been repaired and painted, make a cushion of foam rubber and cover it in a cheery fabric, and you will have a brand new chair or sofa for very little output from the pocketbook—and not too much output of energy either. Spray paints dry so fast that this project can be finished easily in a day.

CANE

11-2

To repair a chair with a cane seat or back is not quite as easy as with wicker, but it really is not the impossible job that most people think.

There are two basic types of chairs that have cane seats. One type of seat has *grooves* all around the frame, and the other type has *holes drilled* all around the frame (Fig. 11-2). No matter which type you are planning to restore (Figs. 11-3 and 11-4), the first rule is the same. *The chair must always be completely refinished before caning,* and the inside rim of the seat must be reglued with epoxy and held with clamps until throughly dry.

Through years of use and constant pressure on the cane, particularly on the frame with drilled holes, the cane is constantly pulling against the frame, tending to cause it to split (Fig. 11-5). When the chair has been refinished, and the frame strengthened in this manner, then comes the moment of decision. Are you going to attempt to cane it yourself, or are you going to hire someone else to do it?

If you live in a town of moderate size or larger, the Association for the Blind does caning; sometimes the Goodwill Industries and other organizations that hire the handicapped do this kind of work. It is difficult to find an individual craftsman who does caning anymore.

If the town where you live is small, you will be more likely to have someone who does caning professionally. However, even if you are lucky enough to find such a person, it is not cheap to having caning done professionally. The price varies from 1¢ to 10¢ a hole, and if you ever stop to count the number of holes in the seat or seat and back of that chair that needs re-caning, it is worth the effort to do it yourself.

Caning is not hard! It requires patience, and it makes the fingers very sore. In a way it's like knitting a pair of argyle socks for the first time; in the beginning, you'll spend more time ripping your stitches than you'll spend actually knitting.

For this job, especially for the first time, a kit is the only answer. The best kit I have found is by mail order from the *Newell Workshop,* 19 Blaine Avenue, Hinsdale, Il. 60521. Unless it is ordered by air mail, allow several weeks for delivery. The kit can be ordered before starting to refinish the chair; and by the time you are ready to start caning, the kit will have arrived. This kit costs $3 plus postage.

The reason for recommending this one over others is *not* the type of cane or price or tools that come with it, but the instruction book. The step-by-step instructions are given with clear illustrations that even people (not like you, of course) with thick heads and six thumbs on each hand can follow.

The one pitfall to avoid when you actually start the caning (and this is not mentioned in any book of instructions that I have ever seen) is that when one is weaving the cane from one side of the chair seat to the other *on the underneath side,* watch carefully, so that the cane does not loop around the rungs of the chair. This sounds a little like saying, "Don't put beans up your nose," but it can happen; and when it does, it means pulling the entire row out and starting over again.

The other pitfall which is not stressed strongly enough in the instruction books is to have your rows perfectly straight in the very beginning step. If the first rows are not perfectly straight and parallel to each other, the final rows will also be off kilter, which is the last thing you want after all the time, and sore fingers, spent on the new chair seat.

If the chair seat is *grooved* rather than having holes drilled all around the seat, then cane webbing can be bought by the sheet in widths up to 24 inches and lengths up to 35 inches, and these are also available from the Newell Workshop and come complete with instruction books.

The same basic rules apply: refinish the frame first. Obviously, the cane in sheets is not as difficult as weaving your own and can be recommended highly.

11-3

11-4

In metropolitan areas, sheets of plastic cane in pure white can be bought. This is very effective on a brightly painted chair or stool for a modern look.

RUSH

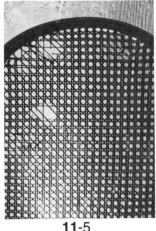

11-5

If the chair to be repaired has a rush seat and is an antique, most dealers recommend that the seat *not* be replaced unless it is absolutely impossible to repair (Fig. 11-6). Naturally, the

11-6

antique value of the chair goes down as soon as the original rush is replaced. If there are only a few loose strands of rush, repairing this is simple procedure.

All you need is Elmer's glue to replace the loose strands of rush to their proper place. When the glue has dried, use a clear shellac to retop the whole seat, and that is all there is to that!

12
Protecting Refinished Surfaces

All of a sudden, after having spent hours and hours refinishing your table, chest, or dry sink, it looks so beautiful that you are afraid to use it—much less let anyone put down a glass without a coaster. If you will follow the instructions given below, the lack of a coaster will never be a worry for you.

PROTECTIVE FINISHES

If the piece which you have completed is an antique which has been *refinished naturally* (not painted), the shellac and wax treatment mentioned in Chapter 3 is the best possible protection for serving tops. There is nothing—not even alcohol—that should leave any mark at all on this type of finish; but, if by chance you find a circle after the guests have gone, the way to remove it is just by rubbing with a soft, clean dry cloth.

If the furniture to be made damage-proof has been *painted* instead of having a natural finish, you will need the following items: pumice powder, clear flat varnish, linseed oil, a brush for the varnish, and a rag for the oil and powder.

You will first coat the painted top with two coats of the clear, flat varnish, allowing the first coat to dry completely before applying the second. When the second coat of varnish has also dried thoroughly, you will then take your clean rag and dampen it slightly with the linseed oil; now dip the dampened rag in the pumice powder mixture. Keep rubbing until all traces of oiliness have disappeared.

When this is dry, you will have the best possible waterproof, alcohol-proof, any-proof (except cigarette, of course) finish that it is possible to have without using synthetics. The beauty of this treatment is that by using the flat varnish, nothing will show. The top of your furniture will not look any different from the sides or legs. The protective coating is completely invisible.

There are other kinds of protective coatings for serving tops that are made of synthetics. These are in a class by themselves.

Decorative Synthetics

Con-Tact Con-Tact, one of several brand names, is a material that has been on the market for years and comes in an almost unlimited choice of color and design. Con-Tact is a plastic material with an adhesive backing. Con-Tact is sold by the yard and by the piece. It can be used as shelf paper, wallpaper (although a little expensive unless you are doing just one wall for special effect), table topping, or as a new finish for any piece of furniture that is flat. It can even be used on floors.

Con-Tact also comes in natural wood finishes; its *heavy duty* strips and rolls, which are 30 inches wide, even simulate natural brick and bamboo, with a three-dimensional quality. If a piece of furniture needs temporary refinishing until your time permits wood stripping, Con-Tact is the answer to your problem.

The protective paper backing is marked off in inches for easy measurement and cutting. Cut it to the correct size for the surface to be covered, remove the protective paper backing, and lay it down. There is certainly nothing hard about this, but one word of warning. Con-Tact really sticks! So go slowly and place it right the first time. The adhesive on the back does not permit sliding around as wallpaper paste does, although small sections at a time can be lifted off and straightened out.

If you have a large area to cover, remove only a foot or so of the protective backing at a time. Anything flat, like a table knife, is useful for smoothing and eliminating small air bubbles. If you get one side crooked, zip it up and start all over again. When Con-Tact has been applied properly without wrinkles, and with the design going the right way, some tiny air bubbles may insist on being there; if they are not too big, just pop them with a straight pin and press down with your finger. It will never show.

Con-Tact is not limited in its use to tabletops. Whole pieces of furniture have been covered with it—bookcases, record players, dressers, anything at all except a turned leg or arm of a chair. Con-Tact can't be used for this purpose simply because of the nature of the material. Any *flat* surface may be covered, and this material will hold up for years. It can be washed, and no liquid will ever mar it. If put on smoothly, the solid colors will look just like paint, even at close range.

Fiberglass This is a product that has become extremely popular in the last few years. If you have a table frame of either wood or wrought iron, and do not want to go to the trouble of making a mosaic tile top, but still want something durable enough for outdoor use and handsome enough for indoor use, fiberglass is the easy answer to all your problems.

The designs in fiberglass that are available today are a far cry from the first kinds that came out years ago. Originally, this product was used primarily for room dividers in beauty parlors, for awnings, and as patio roofs.

The fiberglass for you is not the old heavy corrugated plastic in awful colors. What you need for your tabletop is the new ⅛-inch thick (or thin) smooth flat fiberglass. This material may be bought at any of the larger lumberyards. Some hardware stores also carry it, but the selection here will be limited in both color and pattern.

There are a number of patterns to be found in fiberglass. There are basketweaves, city scenes, and designs which are

Oriental in feeling with butterflies, leaves, or ferns laminated into the material. These are perfectly good for a porch or patio. Aside from being the simplest solution in the world for a handsome tabletop, this material is absolutely indestructible!

If you decide to use fiberglass for a tabletop, the first thing that you need to do, as usual, is either paint or refinish the table frame. When the frame is ready, measure for the exact size of the fiberglass that you will need, go to the lumberyard, buy the correct size, bring it home, and place it on the table frame. What could be easier than that!

Plexiglas Plexiglas is different from fiberglass in that it is not made from fibers. Plexiglas is a hard clear plastic molded in sheets. This material is so hard that it is used for cockpits of airplanes. Although this material does come in colors, to me, the clear "glass" is the most beautiful. This material is manufactured by Rohm and Haas Co., of Philadelphia. Plexiglas has become so popular with do-it-yourselfer's that Rohm and Haas has produced instructional booklets and special tools for working with this material.

Plexiglas is a good solution for a wrought iron tabletop where you want something clear like glass but are afraid to use glass because of breakage.

Marble

Using a piece of marble for a tabletop is just as easy as using fiberglass or Plexiglas; for again, all you need to do is measure, cut, and put in place. In this case, though, you will have to have a professional do the cutting for you.

With the use of marble, handsome furniture can be made

12-1

from the most unlikely pieces. The practical coffee table shown in Figure 12-1 was made from a raggedy needlepoint piano bench found in a second hand furniture store—minus most of the stuffing. The frame was refinished and the marble was simply set on top of the frame. Marble does have an advantage in that its weight is so great that it does not have to be set *in* a frame to stay in place. It can be placed right on top and will be perfectly steady.

In caring for marble, remember that it is *not* indestructible. A wet glass will leave a permanent ring unless the marble has some protective finish on it. The best possible protection is *Simoniz © car wax*. This gives a beautiful polish—the same as on your car. Simonizing will keep you from pushing the panic button whenever a guest inadvertently puts a wet glass on your table.

If you should choose to use any or all of the above mentioned methods for furniture tops, you ought to have the most "all-proof" tables in the world, and the best part of any of these solutions to the spilled-liquid problem is that none of them need to look the least bit utilitarian. You will be one of the lucky ones who has the unbeatable combination of utility and beauty.

13
New Materials for Refinishing

Refinishing at home has become such a popular American pastime in the last few years that there is a wealth of new materials on the market today to help make even the worst job of restoration not quite as painful as it might have been at one time.

The most spectacular additions to the refinishing and restoring of furniture are not so much in the area of removing old finishes, because the use of sandpaper and elbow grease never changes. The spectaculars are in the wide variety of choice of new stains, paints, and varnishes for the actual refinishing of your furniture.

It is no longer necessary to have to mix your own stain to get the correct color—or the color you want, which is the same thing. Most of the time you can hie yourself to the nearest hardware store and have a choice among as many as 8 to 10 different colors of stains in a range from "black bark" to "birch" which is almost white. There are even a few varnishes with the stain already mixed, but these are mostly the high-gloss varnishes.

STAINS AND VARNISH

Satin-Sheen Stains® come in a variety of colors. There is a pigmented type; brush on and let sit four or five minutes and wipe off. It is outstanding for sun fastness and natural color and can be used on any type of wood. (Glidden-Spred Paints, 2001 W. Moyamensing Ave., Philadelphia, PA 19145)

Min-Wax Stains come in a wide range of colors of natural wood tones. As with most stains, they are very easily applied. (Miniwax Co., Inc., Oak Street, Delawanna, NJ 07014)

Stain 'n Buff is different from the others since it comes in a tube. Because of its waxy quality, it may be used to fill in scratches. If the color does not quite match, combinations of colors can be mixed easily; simply apply with a soft dry cloth. This product is not recommended for large pieces of furniture because it is more expensive than ordinary stains; however, it is excellent for picture frames, wooden bowls, etc. (Rub 'n Buff Division, American Art Clay Co., Inc. Box 68163, Indianapolis, IN 46268)

Sherwin-Williams Wood Stain® is highly recommended for three reasons: the colors are excellent; it stains and seals at the same time, so no sealer is necessary; it is latex and is easily removed from hands and brushes with just ordinary soap and water. (The Sherwin-Williams Co., Cleveland, OH 44101)

Rez Latex Stain® is recommended because of the almost endless variety of colors from which to choose. Aside from the ordinary wood colors, there is a blue, olive, sage, platinum, and rose which are attractive. Since this also is a latex stain, it is quick drying and easy to clean up afterwards. (PPG Industries, 1 Gateway Center, Pittsburgh, PA 15222)

Satin-Sheen Varnish® dries overnight and gives the appearance of a rubbed finish. One coat is enough. (Glidden-Spred Paints, 2001 W. Moyamensing Ave., Philadelphia, PA 19145)

PAINTS

Shining Armor ® is a quick drying spray enamel; one of the few spray enamels that is excellent for covering Styrofoam® and other plastics. (Illinois Bronze Powder and Paint Co., Lake Zurich, IL 60047)

Wet Paint ® a great new spray enamel that gives a super shiny patent leather finish, is perfect for modern furniture, although the variety of color is somewhat limited. (Illinois Bronze Powder and Paint Co.)

Provincial Color Glaze® comes in an excellent choice of colors and wood tones especially for antiquing furniture. (Martin-Senour Paint Co., 2500 S. Senour Avenue, Chicago, IL 60608)

Frostique pastel paints are used for a lighter look than antiquing and may be bought in kits complete with "frosting." (Martin-Senour)

Old Colonial ® is a semi-gloss enamel that comes in reproductions of colors used in colonial times. It is a superb finish for furniture but more expensive than your average enamel; however, the results that are achieved with this paint are worth the extra price. (Turco Paint and Varnish Co., 2146–50 Norris St., Philadelphia, PA 19125)

TILES AND PLASTICS

American Olean Tile Co. has ceramic tiles in sheets 4 feet square which may be cut to order. This company has stores all over the United States and in the Bahamas. (1723 West North Avenue, Pittsburgh, PA 15233)

American Handicrafts has craft shops all over the United States and handles both ceramic and glass tiles and all the necessary equipment for working with them. (1920 8th Ave., Ft. Worth, TX 76110)

Rohm and Haas Co. manufactures Plexiglas and has booklets for do-it-yourselfers. The booklets are 25c; the plans for projects are 50c. (P. O. Box 9730, Philadelphia, PA 19140)

Ceramic tiles for mosaics may also be purchased from builders' supply houses.

METAL POLISHES

Hagerty's® can't be beat for bad brass! Of course, if the brass is really black and beyond ordinary polish, use *Parson's Sudsy* ® household ammonia to remove all the black. It will just float away. Then use the polish. Both these products may be bought in any supermarket or hardware store.

Boat-Nu, though not a polish, is an excellent product for spraying on brass *after* polishing to prevent tarnish. (Evershine Products, Atlanta, GA 30341)

GLASS AND CERAMIC CLEANER

Polident ®, available at drug stores and generally used to clean false teeth, is fantastic for cleaning the old vases and jars that nothing else will touch—neither vinegar nor Clorox ®. Fill the vase with water and drop in a tablet—next thing you know, it's crystal clear.

14
Identification of Woods

Trying to identify the type of wood used to build a certain piece of furniture is a particularly difficult task for the amateur. It really is not very hard to recognize an oak tree when there are acorns all around or if you have some general idea of the leaf shape; but when that same tree has been converted into a table complete with stain and varnish or maybe even a coat of paint on top, it is hard to know what kind of wood it is.

Raw wood at the lumberyard is fairly easy to identify. Luckily for every potential buyer of new or used furniture, every piece has a back or underside, and there the truth will come to light. For a starter lesson before discussing color or grain, it is a good idea to know something about the hardness of the wood with which you are going to become involved because this factor will make a difference in the approach you take toward refinishing.

Identification of Woods   115

The following chart is from the *Encyclopedia Americana* (Grolier, Inc., New York, NY).

Very Hard	Hard	Soft	Very Soft
Hickory	Cherry	Ponderosa pine	White pine
Hard maple	Oak	Chestnut	Sugar pine
	Beech	Yellow poplar	Spruce
	Birch	Cypress	Red wood
	Long leaf pine	Cedar	
	Ash		
	Walnut		
	Maple		
	Poplar		
	Mahogany		

The woods most generally used in the making of furniture will be the ones discussed here. The varieties are listed alphabetically rather than under headings by characteristic.

CEDAR

In the refinishing of furniture, unless the piece to be restored is a not-very-old blanket chest, you are not likely to run across cedar. As shown on the chart, cedar is soft; it is also a rather unattractive bright pinkish wood. The grain is very much like that of pine (Fig. 14-1). In white pine, however, the grain is only slightly darker than the basic color of the wood, but the grain of cedar is unmistakably distinct. If the blanket chest which you are refinishing is of cedar, paint the outside, but leave the inside alone, for the real value of cedar, as everyone knows, is its moth-preventing scent.

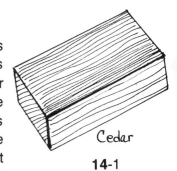

14-1

CHERRY

The soft reddish brown color of cherry is a far cry from the gashes of red in cedar. Cherry is a hardwood from which only fine furniture is made. Many fine antique pieces are of cherry because of its likeness to the very popular and much more expensive mahogany which was so much in demand a century

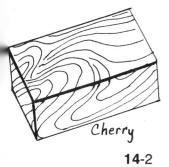

14-2

or more ago. The grain of cherry is a series of fine thin lines (Fig. 14-2). The advertisements seen so often in the newspapers about "fruitwood" furniture usually do *not* mean cherry. They mean *hackberry* which is more like elm; but since it produces a berry, it can be called fruitwood. It is then stained to resemble cherry. Any type of finish may be used on cherry—oil, shellac-wax, or varnish. There is nothing to hide with this beautiful wood.

MAHOGANY

A lumberman once said that he would just as soon buy gold as mahogany. This wood is probably the most popular of all in furniture making. Although the finish of mahogany changes with the years and fashion in furniture, its beauty of color and grain, and its hardness and durability keep it in use. The true natural color of mahogany is reddish tan to brown. Most people are inclined to think of mahogany as being dark brown, almost black in color, because for a number of years dark mahogany furniture was the vogue. The grain of mahogany, rather than being in a distinct line or pattern, such as pine or cedar, is "feathery" and close (Fig. 14-3). It goes without saying that it would be nothing short of sacrilege to do anything to mahogany but finish it naturally without any stain at all.

14-3

OAK

The less said about oak the better. You will not find a more durable wood for funiture, with the exception of ash. White oak is seldom seen in new furniture—with the exception of very informal furnishings for dens or boys' rooms. If you are planning on refinishing a chair or sideboard circa 1900, more than likely it will be oak. The Victorians loved this ponderous wood (Fig. 14-4). The color of white oak is really yellow rather than white, but it can hardly be called tan. The grain of oak is denser than that of mahogany. The wood is so hard that it does not take a stain or natural finish easily. But I recommend Min-Wax in a light walnut stain for a beautiful finish. If it is a

14-4

piece that requires stripping, and you are not feeling particularly ambitious, paint it.

POPLAR

This wood is easily recognizable a half-mile away because of its distinctive greenish color (Fig. 14-5). The wood is soft and has a grain similar to pine, but you would never confuse it with pine because of its color. This wood must be bleached before any refinishing can be done. If it has been used in combination with pine (which it probably has), it should be bleached and then given the same treatment as the pine. You are not likely to find a whole piece of furniture made just from poplar. If you do, the easiest way to treat it is to paint it.

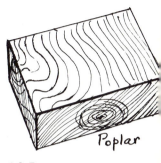
14-5

SUGAR MAPLE

This wood (Fig. 14-6) is lighter in color than any of those listed above. Sugar maple has a yellow cast to it and could be classified in color as yellowish-brown, or honey colored if you prefer. This wood, which is used for more casual furniture than mahogany, walnut, or cherry, has a coarser heavier grain than any of the others. Maple is a hard, durable wood and should be given a natural finish with wax and shellac. However, if the color should be a little light for your taste, it would be a good idea to use a walnut or other dark stain before finishing with shellac and wax.

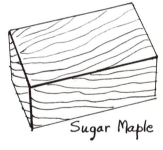
14-6

WALNUT

This beautiful fine-grained hardwood for years was grossly misunderstood. For during the post-Civil War era on through the twenties, the "best" black walnut furniture came complete with hideous black staining. Actually, there is nothing black about black walnut except the hull on the nut that falls from the tree. The natural wood is a rich warm brown with a very fine grain (Fig. 14-7). In refinishing furniture made from black

14-7

walnut, this wood should never be stained. An oil finish is excellent for a modern look, or for a more traditional piece, the shellac-wax is good. At the present time, black walnut has probably replaced mahogany as the most expensive wood of all.

WHITE PINE

14-8

This very soft, easy-to-handle wood is probably the most easily identifiable of all the furniture woods. Nearly all the unpainted furniture produced today is of white pine. The grain of the wood is fairly strong and clear (Fig. 14-8), but not unattractive. This porous wood takes staining very well; and, because of its almost dead white color, it should be stained before finishing. Pine, like maple, is generally used in the more casual furniture; however, if there is a really excellent store in your area for unfinished furniture, this is the kind of place from which you can make your own antiques as mentioned earlier in this book. Use a walnut or mahogany stain on the unpainted four-poster bed with the tester, and you will have a real treasure—an antique of the future.

YELLOW PINE

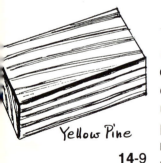

14-9

Yellow pine has the same type of grain as the white pine, but it is deeper in color than its relative and much harder and more durable than white pine. (Fig. 14-9). Almost all the antique country and survival furniture is built of yellow pine, or pine used in combination with other woods such as poplar. For proper refinishing, the fine old yellow pine found in antiques must *never* be painted. Most of the time you will find yourself removing layers of paint to restore the natural yellow pine finish. A wax-shellac finish is mandatory with yellow pine.

On the other hand, if you have been fortunate enough to find an antique corner cupboard or hutch which has the original *buttermilk* based paint on it, never ever remove this. Buttermilk based paint is usually brick red or dark green and has a dull, rough primitive look. This old type of paint adds enormously to the antique value of the piece and any antique dealer would recognize it.

CURLS AND BURLS

You might have a piece of furniture made some time between 1850 and 1880 which you are certain is walnut or mahogany, but in which the grain just is not true. Rather than feathers or fine lines, you may find that your table or chest seems to be of curly wood (Fig. 14-10). Most people call this curly patterned wood "burled"; and in some cases, this is correct, but most of the time this is wrong.

14-10

In the first place, what is commonly called "burl" is generally "butt." Both butt and burl woods are used for veneers and for decorative panels on the front of furniture; both are highly decorative and "swirly" in design, and neither butts nor burls are limited to one kind of wood, though maple burls are very common. Did you ever hear of "waterfall" mahogany? A waterfall panel was made by combining burls in a pattern to look like a waterfall. Most people would not be caught dead with it around the house today, but 30 or 40 years ago the most expensive bed or chifforobe was not complete without its waterfall panel.

The difference between the two is in the part of the tree from which they come. A butt is stump wood at the point where the trunk divides. A burl is simply a thick growth of layers of wood over a defect in the tree. Sometimes these layers occur even over a layer of bark.

Empire furniture of the middle 1800s used burl and butt extensively in tabletops and for decorative panels on drawers and cupboard doors.

15
Care of Antiques

Antiques are like people. The older ones necessarily require more care than the young ones. The principle reason that antiques require a little more special care than newer furniture is that they are more sensitive to change of temperature and humidity than new furniture.

Obviously, any piece of furniture classified as "antique" was built before the days of central heating. It is not the old-fashioned steam heat with radiators that is so bad for old furniture, although that is bad enough, but it is the hot air vents that will really do in a good piece of antique furniture.

As with most things, "an ounce of prevention . . ." holds true in the care of antiques. In the summertime, there is no problem because nothing is better for old furniture than a humid day. Of course, if your home is in the Amazon jungle, you have a different type of problem—rotting rather than splitting. The majority of people in this country do not live in jungle situations (at least as far as the climate is concerned); and if they do, they have air-conditioning, which is just as bad as dry heat in the winter. The proper thing to do is to simulate as much as possible the ideal climate for your good furniture.

HELPFUL HINTS

Rule number one is to *keep the thermostat down to a reasonable level*. Mid-sixty is not bad at all. Rule number two which should not even need to be written is *don't place your furniture over an air vent if you can help it*. If furniture has to be placed near or over an air vent, place a pan of water under the furniture to provide enough humidity to counteract the dry heat. This will help to keep the wood from drying and splitting.

If you have old-fashioned radiators in your house, nearly all of them have a water pan underneath the cover of the radiator. Keep this pan filled all the time in each room of the house, and it will not be necessary to put pans of water under the furniture.

For all who own a baby grand piano, the ounce of prevention is to lift the lid and place small containers of water right on the sounding board inside the piano (Fig. 15-1). This will help prevent cracking of the sounding board as well as protect the case of the piano. You will be surprised to see how quickly the water evaporates, especially during the winter.

People who are great with house plants will not find it necessary to keep the furniture watered. Just keeping the plants watered will provide enough humidity for the room. However, this does not mean that one small African violet will provide enough moisture for an entire room.

15-1

Keep your antiques well waxed. Do not use spray waxes on this fine furniture. Use Butcher's paste wax and elbow grease. Buff the wax well. This is not easy to do, but who wants a sticky tabletop that is a magnet for dust?

If it is already too late for that ounce of prevention, and you have found veneer that has buckled, or even worse, a beautiful solid piece of wood that has split all the way down the middle, then there is nothing to do but repair it. The extent of the repair, naturally, depends on the extent of the damage.

If there is only a slight crack, this can be filled in with wax and darkened with shoe polish, and no one will be the wiser. This works better than those wax pencils with stains built in them that are found in hardware stores for covering scratches. If the split is very wide, then wood filler will have to be used and stained to match the rest of the wood. This is a little more difficult because it will require sanding, and that sanding means a small refinishing job to match the old finish as closely as possible.

The only two things needed to repair split veneer are epoxy glue and "C" clamps. Apply the glue; apply the clamp; let dry; and *voila!* it's finished.

One last word of advice—if your finished project does not turn out as well as you had hoped, please don't take it out on the rest of the family!

Index

Page numbers in **boldface** *type indicate illustrations.*

American Handicrafts, 47, 63, 87, 112
American Home, 47
American Home Crafts, 87
American Olean Tile Co., 65, 112
Ammonia, household, 21, 57, 58, 113
Andirons, 58
Antique(s)
  antiquing versus, 43
  buying, 23–24
  care of, 120–22
  chair with rush seat, 103–**104**
  choice of, for refinishing, 6, 7
  picture frames, 72
  pine, 118
    yellow, 118–19
  tiles, 69–71
  trays, 81, 82, 89
  unscrupulous "producing" of, 34
  See also Country furniture; Victorian furniture
Antique look, on tray or wastebasket, 86
Antiquing, 43–54
Antiquing glaze, 49–51
Antiquing kits, 51–52
Apartment, work area in, 14–15
Appliquéing of print, 84, **85**
Association for the Blind, 101
Attic, work area in, 14

Ball and Brass Works, 57
Basement, work area in, 14, 16
Beading, on gold leaf frames, 74, 75
Beds
  brass, 58–59
  iron, with brass trim, 59–60

124 Furniture Refinishing

Blanket chest, 115
Bleaching, 26
  of poplar, 32, 117
Boat-Nu, 58
Brass, 55–60
  beds of, 58–59
  hardware of, 55–58
  lamp of, 96
  polish for, 57, 113
  trim of, 57–60
  See also Knobs; Pulls
Brasso, 57
Bronzing powder, 76
Brushes
  paint, 21, 26, 28
  for painting with design or stencil, 86, 87
Buffing, 41
Burls in wood, 119
Burnt sienna oil paint, 35
Burnt (Turkey) umber, 49
Butcher's wax, 41, 122
Butt, 119
Buttermilk based paint, 118

Cane, repairing, **100**, 101, **102**, **103**
Catalogs, for hardware, 57
Cedar, **115**
Cement, for tiles, 70
Ceramic cleaner, 113
Ceramic tiles, 64–65
  availability of, 112
  soaking, 66
Chairs, 99–104
  See also Seats
Cherry, 115–**16**
Chippendale furniture, 24
Chippendale tray, **82**
Cleaning
  brass bed, 59
  brass hardware, 57
  ceramics, 113
  glass, 113
  See also Washing
Con-Tact, 90, 106–107
Copper tub, **60**

Corn husk, seats of, 9
Corner cupboard, 118
Country furniture, 6, 23–**25**, 36, 118
Curls in wood, 119

Decorating
  with fabrics, 89–91
  with painted designs, 46–49
Decorative synthetics, 106–108
Decoupage, 82
  on small furniture, 91
Design
  disastrous, 45
  good, 8
  mosaic, 62, 64
  painted, decorating with, 46–49
  painting with, 86–89
  ugly, 9–10
Detergents, 21
Dipper, 5
  for brass beds, 58
Door Stores, Inc., 78
Doors, refinishing, 37–38
  See also Hinges
Dovetailing, **36**
Drawers, refinishing, 35–36
Dry sink, 6, **7**, 24
  refinishing, 35–38
  taking down, 28–35
Drying time
  for antiquing, 50–51
  for painted designs, 46–48
  for shellac, 40, 41
  after washing, 30, 40, 46
  with shellac solvent, 32

Early American furniture, 24
Edging, for mosaics, 68–69
Electrical wiring of lamp, 96–98
Electricity, care in use of, 14, 16
Elmer's glue, 21, 35
Epoxy, 21, 35

Fabrics, decorating with, 89–91
Fiberglass, to protect surface, 107–108

Fibre-seal, 87, 88
File, for repairs, 34
Finishes
  natural, 39–42
  oil, 42
  protective, 105
  removing 23–28, 44–45
  wax-shellac, 39–42
  for wood frames, 78
Fireplace facing, replacing tiles around, 69
Frames, picture; *See* Picture frames
Frostique, 51, 52, 112
Fruitwood, 116
Furniture
  early 1900's, 6–7, 44, 116
  fine period, 8–9, 24
  "horrendous," 44–45
  modern, 6–7, 44, 116
  small, decoupage on, 91–93
  "taking down," 23–38
  ugly, 9–10
  See also Antiquing; Refinishing; Unpainted furniture; Victorian furniture

Garage, work area in, 14
Glass cleaner, 113
Glass topped tables, 60
Glaze(s)
  antiquing, 49–52
  over tray design, 88
Glidden's, 34
Gloves, rubber, 27
Glue, 21, 35
Gold enamel paint, 76, 84
Gold leaf, 48–49
  plaster and, over solid wood frames, 78–79
Gold leaf frames, 73–77
Goodwill Industry, 7, 101
Grout, 67–69
  painted, 69

Hackberry, 116
Hagerty's, 113

Hardware, 36–37
  brass, 57–58
  sideboard, 45
  See also Knobs; Pulls
Hardwoods, 26, 115
Heat, effect of, on antiques, 120–21
Hepplewhite, 24
Hinges, 36, 57
  brass, 57
  cleaning, 57
  "H" or "L and H" black hammered, 36, **38**
  in hanging doors, 38
  invisible, 37
Horton Brasses A. J., 57
Humidity, for antiques, 121
Hutch, 118

Iron furniture, 59–60
Ivory, 29

Jack knife, 21, 26
Janitor in a Drum, 21
Jars, for storage, **18**–19
Johnson's wax, 41

Kits, 5–6
  antiquing, 45, 51–52
  caning, 101
  tile, 64
Knife
  jack, 21, 26
  putty, 21, 26
Knobs
  door, 38
    wooden versus brass, 38
  for pulls, 36
    wooden versus brass, 36

Lacquer, spray, to prevent tarnish, 58
Lamps
  making wooden, 97–98
  restoring old, 94–97
Lestoil, 21
Lighting, for work area, 16–19

Linseed oil
  boiled, for wax-shellac finish, 39–40
  boiled and raw, for oil finish, 42
Lux, 29

Mahogany, **116**
  curls and burls and "waterfalls" in, 119
Mahogany stain, 66
Mahogany varnish, 44
Maple, sugar, **117**
Marbelized finish, 51–52
Marble table top, 52, 54, 108
Martin Senour Paints, 51
Metal polishes, 113
  See also Brass, polishes for
Min-Wax, 41
  oil finish of, 78
Min-Wax Stains, 111
Modern furniture, 6–7, 44, 116
Molding, for mosaics, 68–69
Mosaics, 61–71
Mr. Clean, 21

Nails
  headless, 36
  storing, **18**–19
Newell Workshop, 101, 102
Nickel finish, on lamp, 96, 97
Nimocks, Patricia, 81, 91

Oak, **116**–17
  yellow, 44
Oil
  boiled linseed, 39–40, 42
  machine, for cleaning, 37
  removing, 26
Oil finish, 42
Oil Finish, 78
Oil paints
  for antiquing, 49
  for decorations, 47–48
  for stains, 35
Old Colonial, 112
Overtone, 48–51
  applying, 50–51

  for decoupage, 84
  hardware and, 55
  painted designs and, 48
  painting without, 52–54
  using, 49–51
Oxalic acid, 26, 32

Paint(s)
  available, 112
  buttermilk based, on yellow pine antique, 118–19
  on iron furniture, 59
  oil, 35, 47–49
  "wet," glossy, 86, 112
Paint remover, 21, 26–28, 30–31
Paint scraper, **21,** 26
Paintbrushes, 21, 26, 28
Painted surface, protective finish for, 106
Painted designs, 46–49
Painting
  antiquing and, 43–54
  base coat, 46
  with design or stencil, 86–89
  final coat, 46, 47
  of furniture, decision on, 11
  before laying mosaic, 66
  without overtone, 52–54
  of wrought iron furniture, 59
Parson's Sudsy ammonia, 57, 113
  See also Ammonia
Patina, removing old, 9
Patterns
  for painted decorations, 47
  for painted designs, 87
Pegboard, for supplies, 17–18
Period furniture, 8–9, 24
Picture frames, 72–80
  gold leaf, 74–77
  shadow, 80
  solid wood, using plaster and gold leaf over, 78–79
  unpainted, 79–80
  wood veneer, 77–78

Pine
  dark stain for, 35
  unpainted furniture of, 11
  white, **118**
    stripping, 26
  yellow, **118**–19
    poplar next to, 32, 117
Planters, lamps as, 94–96
Plastics, materials available in, 112
Plaster, on frames, 73, 74
  regilding, 76–77
  repairing, 74–75
  on solid wood, 78–79
Plaster of paris, working with, 74–75
Plexiglas, 108
Plywood, for supplies, **17**–18
Polident, 113
Polishes, metal, 113
  brass, 57, 113
Polishing, 41
Poplar, **117**
  bleaching, 26, 32
Primer coat of paint, 46
Print, for decoupage, 82, **84, 85**
Provincial Color Glaze, 112
Pulls
  brass, 57–58
  cleaning, 57–58
  door, 38
  drawer, 36
  drop, on sideboards, 45
  elaborate or plain, 55, **56,** 57
Putty, wood, 34
Putty knife, 21, 26

Quik-i-Poxy, 21, 35

Rags, 21
  oily, throwing away, 40, 42
  polishing, 41
Razor blades, 26
Red Devil, 26
Refinishing, 24–38
  of dry sink, 35–38
  materials available for, 110–13

over-, 9
  protecting surfaces after, 105–109
  what not to, 8–11
  why, what, and when, 3–12
Regilding of plaster, 76–77
  See also Gold leaf
Remover, paint and varnish, 21, 26–28
  homemade, to supplement commercial, 31
  need to sand after, 32–33
  using, 30–31
Removing finishes, 23–28
Repairs, 122
  of drawers, 35–36
  after stripping, 33–35
Reproductions, 36
  hardware, 57
  versus restoration, 34, 36–37
Restoration
  of gold leaf frame, 74–75
  hardware for, 55
  of natural finish, 39–42
  of old lamps, 94–97
  of picture frames, 78
  versus reproductions, 34, 36–37
Revere tray, **82,** 87
Rez Latex Stain, 111
Rohm and Haas Co., 108, 112
Rope, seats of, 9
Run 'n Buff, 48, 49, 51, 111
Rush seat, 9, **10,** 103–**104**

Salvation Army, 7
Sander
  electric, on softer woods, 26
  hand and electric, 19–**20**
  orbital, 19, 20
  renting, 28
  round, 20
  vertical, 20
Sanding
  before antiquing, 46
  after shellacing, 41
  in "taking down" process, 33

Sandpaper, 19, 27, 33
Satin-Sheen Stains, 111
Satin-Sheen Varnish, 111
Scraper, paint, **21,** 26
Screws, storing, **18**–19
Scrub brush, 26
Scrub bucket, zinc, 26
Sealer
    shellac as, 66
    silicone, 68
    tile, 68
Seats
    corn husk, 9
    rush, 9, **10,** 103–**104**
    woven, 9, **10**
Secretaries, 55, **56**
Shellac
    applying, 40
    four pound cut, 40
    as sealer, 66
Shellac solvent, 27, 40
    washing with, 32
Sheraton furniture, 24
Sherwin-Williams, 34, 111
Shining Armor, 112
Shoe polish, brown paste, for finish, 78
Sideboards, 44–45
Silicone sealer, 68
Simoniz car wax, 109
Soap, washing with, 29–30
Sobo glue, 21, 35
Softwoods, 115
    stripping of, 26
Solvent, shellac, 27, 32, 40
Sponges, 21
Stain 'n Buff, 34, 111
Stains
    availability of commercial, 34, 111
    bleeding, 66
    for picture frames, 78
    on picture frame, removing, 77–78
    in refinishing, 34–35
    for repairs, 34–36
Steel wool, 21, 27, 58

Stencil, painting with, 86–89
Stone chisel, 67
Storage, of work supplies, 16–19
Strip-Eze, 26
Stripping, 23–33
    of brass bed, 58
    professional, 5, 58
    tools and supplies for, 23–28
Sunlight, in bleaching, 32
Supplies
    furniture refinishing, 19–22, 24–28
    mosaic, 62–65
    work area for, 16–19
Survival furniture, 23, 118
Synthetics, decorative, 106–108

Table, drop leaf, 24
Tabletops
    fiberglass for, 108
    marble, 52, 54, 108–109
    mosaics for, 61–62
"Taking down" furniture, 23–28
Tarnish, preventing, 58
Tea, immersing print in, 82
Tile(s)
    antique, 69–71
    availability of, 112
    mosaic, 61–66
        soaking of, 66–67
Tile adhesive, 67
Tile nippers, 67
Tole, 9
    tray, 81, 89
Tools, 19–22, 26–28
    work area for, 16–19
Tracing paper, 87–88
Trays, decorating, 81–89
    Chippendale and Revere, 82, 87
    tole, 81, 89
Trim, brass, 57–60
Trisodium phosphate, 26, 31
Turpentine, 21
    with boiled linseed oil, 39–40, 42
    to remove wax and oil, 26

Unpainted furniture, 6, 8, 11–12, 118
Unpainted picture frames, 79–80
Utility room, work area in, 14

Varnish(es)
  availability of, 111
  in oil finish, 42
  over oil painted decoration, 48
  over paint, 47
  overtone and, 50–51
  spar, 52
  spray, 48
  Satin-Sheen, 111
  as tile sealer, 68
Varnish remover, 21, 26
Veneer
  repairing split, 122
  soaking off, in water, 77–78
  wood, picture, frames with, 77–78
Victorian furniture, 7, 8
  late, 44
  oak used for, 116
  picture frames, 73, 78
  washstand, 52, **54**
Vinegar, as antidote, 27

Wall hanging, tile, 71
Walnut, **117**–18
  with black stain, 44
  finish for, 78
  unpainted furniture of, 11–12
Washing of wood, 46
  with shellac solvent, 32
  with soap, 29–31
  See also Cleaning
Washstand, Victorian, 52, **54**
Wastebaskets, decorating, 81–91
  fabrics for, **89, 90,** 91
Wax(es), 41
  applying, in refinishing, 41
  Butcher's, 41, 122
  removing, 26
  Simoniz car, 109
Wax-shellac finish, 39–42
Wet paint, 86, 112
Wicker furniture, 99–100
Wood(s)
  butt, burls, and curls in, 119
  checking quality of, 23
  green (poplar), 26, 32, **117**
  identification of, 114–19
  for repairs, 34–35
    carving, 34
    matching color of, 34–35
Wood filler, 33–34, 36
Wood putty, 34
Wood veneer frames, 77–78
Work area, setting up, 14–22
Wrought iron furniture, 60

Zip-Strip, 26

Nina Joyner, who was born in the South, has lived with antiques all her life. When she was growing up and the family needed furniture, they either went antiquing or had the local cabinetmaker copy an antique that was too expensive to buy. This was during the depression, and at that time antiques were plentiful and cheaper than new furniture.

When Nina got married, her husband was a medical resident earning the magnificent sum of $50 a month. This is when the refinishing projects began. The Joyners found it was cheaper to buy country antiques and refinish them than to buy new furniture (even at chain department stores).

Nina's first book on the subject of refinishing, *Furniture Refinishing at Home,* was written because at that time there were no books on refinishing furniture for the average amateur who had neither money for antiques nor space for a workshop.

At this time Nina was living in a Philadelphia suburb. *Furniture Refinishing at Home* was given a good review in a local paper, "The Main Line Chronicle." Shortly after this, Mrs. Joyner was hired by the "Chronicle" to do feature writing, which she did until 1969.

In 1972 the Joyners moved to Pittsburgh where they now live in the country and are again refinishing furniture and writing about their work.

Mrs. Joyner's husband is a well known cardiologist. She has one daughter, Glenn, at the University of South Carolina, and a son, Courtney, at home who is in 10th grade at Sewickley Academy.

Taking care of three dogs, a vegetable garden, and writing, besides entertaining both friends and doctors who come to Pittsburgh to lecture, keeps her schedule full—but allows time for bridge, which she loves.

The Joyners have a house in South Carolina where they spend their summers, living off the sea, fishing, crabbing, and shrimping. Even there on a rainy day, there is furniture to be refinished and writing to be done.